80, 140, 198
204, 217, 226
234, 245, 256

INCEST: THE LAST TABOO

GARLAND REFERENCE LIBRARY
OF SOCIAL SCIENCE
(VOL. 143)

INCEST: THE LAST TABOO
An Annotated Bibliography

Rick Rubin
Greg Byerly

GARLAND PUBLISHING, INC. • NEW YORK & LONDON
1983

Library of Congress Cataloging in Publication Data

Rubin, Rick, 1949–
  Incest, the last taboo.

  (Garland reference library of social science ;
v. 143)
  Includes indexes.
    1. Incest—United States—Abstracts.   I. Byerly,
Greg, 1949–   . II. Title. III. Series.
HQ72.U53R8   1983   306.7'77   82-49181
ISBN 0-8240-9185-X

Cover design by Laurence Walczak

Printed on acid-free, 250-year-life paper
Manufactured in the United States of America

CONTENTS

INTRODUCTION

For years the topic of incest was ignored by our society. Perhaps because of the intensity and universality of the incest taboo, researchers, social workers and other health professionals have been reluctant to confront and explore this issue. Only recently has the prevalence and impact of incest on the American family been acknowledged.

Nevertheless, in the last decade the quantity of information found in books, periodicals, and audiovisual materials has increased greatly and the rate of increase continues into the 1980s. A notable example of the proliferation of interest in this field is in the area of dissertations. A search of *Comprehensive Dissertations Index* from 1862 through August, 1982, reveals thirty-four dissertations dealing with some aspect of incest. Of these thirty-four, twenty-four were written since 1979 and sixteen were completed in 1981 alone. Similar dramatic increases are evident in recently published books and articles dealing with the topic of incest. It is clear that as the research and interest in incest expands, the need to exercise bibliographic control over the published material is essential.

This book is a selective, annotated bibliography on incest encompassing psychological, sociological, anthropological, medical, scientific, legal, popular, and literary perspectives. Limited to works primarily concerned with the occurrence or discussion of incest in contemporary American society, the book includes monographs, dissertations, journal articles, and audiovisual materials published or produced in English. Chapters on incest from books of a broader scope are typically not included. Emphasis is on works published in the last ten years although significant monographs, dissertations, and articles published in the 1960s and before have been included.

Items chosen for annotation had, first, to illuminate the contemporary concerns with incest in the United States. Second, they had to be accessible, useful research tools. Except for dissertations, unpublished materials, e.g., conference papers, are not included. Similarly, materials not generally available in the United States are excluded.

Once the bibliographic citation for an article was located in such indexes as *Psychological Abstracts, Sociological Abstracts* and *Index Medicus,* items were personally examined by the compilers. Monographs were located through such compilations as the annual editions of *Books in Print* and the *NUC: Books, Subject.* Comprehensive *Dissertations Index* was used to locate dissertations and as a source for abstracts of dissertations unavailable for inspection. The volume and year of the *Dissertation Abstracts International* volume used follow in parentheses at the end of each abstract.

Various sources were used to locate audiovisual materials and as a source for abstracts of items not available for preview. The volume and year of the index used are listed in parentheses at the end of any summarized abstracts.

The book is divided into eight chapters. Chapter I includes significant monographs and dissertations published since 1960. The next six chapters list journal articles from psychological, sociological and legal, anthropological, medical and scientific, popular, and literary periodicals. The last chapter lists relevant audiovisual materials, including films, video cassettes, and audio recordings.

All entries are descriptively annotated; books and major articles are annotated at greater length. Reviews are also listed, where possible, for books, and each entry includes standard bibliographic information (author, title, place of publication, publisher, dates, and pages). Anonymous entries are listed alphabeticaly by title. Illustrations and bibliographies are indicated. Entries are indexed by author and by subject and personal name. There is also a list of periodicals cited.

The process of selecting materials for inclusion proved to be difficult, especially when articles dealt with closely related but distinct topics. Related topics that fall outside the bibliography's scope include the following:

1. Works that deal primariliy with child abuse or the sexual abuse of children in general, such as Kempe's *Child Sexual Abuse,* or Russell Trainer's *The Lolita Complex.*
2. Works that deal with cultural taboos in general or anthropological works on kinship or marriage such as Freud's

Totem and Taboo or Westermarck's *History of Marriage*.
3. Works that are predominantly historical or are primarily discussions of sexual attitudes, behaviors, or mores involving
   children, such as Florence Rush's *The Best Kept Secret:
   Sexual Abuse of Children*.
4. Works that deal primarily with child pornography.*
5. Works that deal primarily with the Oedipal Complex or Elec-
   tra Complex, such as Humberto Nagera's *Female Victims:
   Sexuality and the Oedipus Complex* or Andre Green's *The
   Tragic Effect: The Oedipus Complex in Tragedy*.
6. Works that deal primarily with nonhuman studies of incest,
   e.g., articles on incest among monkey populations.
7. Fictional works such as Anais Nin's *House of Incest*.

All of the articles selected and annotated were placed into one of
the six chapters listing journal articles. At times this assignment was
arbitrary due to the multidisciplinary nature of the articles. While
some fell clearly into an appropriate chapter, others lacked a clearcut
emphasis. Although this arrangement is intended to be helpful in
providing an overview of general aspects of incest, a detailed subject
index is also provided to allow access to more specific or cross-
disciplinary topics.

In general the following guidelines were used in assigning chapters.

Psychological Articles

This chapter includes articles which focus on the individual
characteristics of participants involved in incestuous activities. The
emphasis is typically on individual offenders or victims of incest,
often as reported in case studies. Descriptions of particular treatment programs, actual therapy, and specific therapeutic approaches
of a non-medical nature are also included.

Sociological and Legal Articles

Articles in this chapter deal with the social dynamics of incest
and focus on the forces in society which promote, treat, or proscribe
incestuous relations. Contemporary societal reactions to incest are

*See Greg Byerly and Rick Rubin, *Pornography*, Garland, 1980.

included, but studies of cultural incest taboos are reserved for the chapter dealing with anthropological articles. Legal aspects of incest and the treatment of both victims and offenders by the justice system are represented in this chapter, as well as articles discussing general theories, broad issues pertaining to incest, and such special approaches to understanding incest as viewing incest through the feminist perspective of male dominance.

Anthropological Articles

This chapter includes articles which deal with the cultural and anthropological aspects of incest, especially in primitive cultures or historical societies. Societal rules regarding marriage prohibitions and attitudes toward exogamy, and the origin and universality of the incest taboo are included, as are articles exploring the relationship between folklore and incest.

Medical and Scientific Articles

These articles focus on the role of physicians, nurses, and other health care professionals in detecting and treating members of the incestuous family. Detailed descriptions of both physical symptoms of incest and the examinations and laboratory tests needed to confirm actual physical sexual abuse in incest cases are summarized. Treatments suggested primarily are concerned with the physical needs of the victims. This chapter also contains articles discussing the genetic aspects of incest, such as physical abnormalities, infant mortality, and IQ depression in children of incestuous relations. The biological basis of the incest taboo and the effects of inbreeding are also included.

Popular Articles

This is the only chapter for which relevant articles were selected based solely on the magazine in which they were printed. Articles from popular magazines, i.e., those readily available at newsstands or indexed in *Readers' Guide to Periodical Literature*, were included in this chapter regardless of what aspect of the incest controversy they dealt with. In most cases, however, the articles concern general issues and topics.

Literary Articles

This chapter contains selected representative examples of contemporary criticism of literary works which use the incest motif, including novels, poetry, and drama. The immense scope of both the use of the incest theme and literary criticism precludes comprehensive coverage. Therefore, the articles are merely intended as an overview of recent critical articles on this topic.

Our purpose in this book is to provide a sharply focused, accessibly annotated bibliography for a broad range of researchers including social workers, psychologists, sociologists, health care professionals, students, and interested laymen who are seeking information about the detection, prevention, and treatment of incest in the United States. It should enable researchers to quickly and efficiently survey the broad range of items published on this topic and to avoid the repetition of duplicated entries in various indexes.

INCEST: THE LAST TABOO

I

MONOGRAPHS AND DISSERTATIONS

1. Allen, Charlotte V. *Daddy's Girl*. New York: Simon and Schuster, 1980. 254 pp.

   Explores through a first-person narrative the struggles of an adult victim of childhood incest. Recounts the family relationships and struggles which led to the incest and concentrates on the internal anxiety of the victim as she fought to maintain emotional balance and self-respect. Also deals with the psychological effects of incest on the subsequent adult sexual attitudes and relations of the victim. (REVIEWS: *Kirkus Reviews*, October 1, 1980, p. 1321; *Library Journal*, December 1, 1980, p. 2492; *Publishers Weekly*, September 5, 1980)

2. Armstrong, Louise. *Kiss Daddy Goodnight: A Speak-out on Incest*. New York: Hawthorne Books, 1978. 256 pp.

   Recounts in anecdotal style the experiences of 183 women who voluntarily offered to be interviewed concerning their previous incestuous relationships. Emphasis is on personal narrative with specific accounts of the sexual activity and feelings experienced by the victims. Includes experiences of father-daughter and brother-sister incest. Observes that incest occurs at every level of society and that common to incest victims is a betrayal of trust. Many victims were angrier at their mothers than their fathers. Recommends that emphasis must be on prevention with special attention focused on the father. Includes bibliography, index and appendix with a national list of facilities with incest treatment programs. (REVIEWS: *Booklist*, July 15, 1978, p. 1706; *Library Journal*, June 15, 1978, p. 1276; *Publishers Weekly*, May 29, 1978, p. 46)

3. Bennett, Michael Harris. "Father-Daughter Incest: A
    Psychological Study of the Mother from an Attachment
    Theory Perspective." Ph.D. dissertation, California
    School of Professional Psychology, 1980. 187 pp.

    Investigates the psychological state of mothers in
    families where father-daughter incest is occurring.
    Results indicate: (1) mothers experienced a greater
    number of actual or threatened separations in childhood;
    (2) mothers exhibited an "intropunitive" style of anger
    expression; and (3) mothers had a lower sense of self-
    esteem. Concludes that future attempts to treat incest
    should include more attention on the mother and the dis-
    ruptive separations in her childhood. (DAI XLI [1980])

4. Brady, Katherine. *Father's Days: A True Story of Incest*.
    New York: Seaview Books, 1979. 216 pp.

    Presents a personal narrative of an incestuous relation-
    ship between father and daughter. Explores in detail
    through dialogue and description the family environment
    and dynamics which encouraged the incestuous relationship.
    The deep internal feelings of the victim are explored as
    her sexuality develops in childhood. The sexual en-
    counters with the father are described as well as how the
    victim adjusted to the incestuous relationship. Also
    covers the subsequent difficulties the victim experienced
    in marriage and child rearing. Emphasizes that the
    victims of incest feel that they are the only ones who
    experience this trauma, while, in fact, their plight is
    a common one. (REVIEWS: *Booklist*, November 1, 1979,
    p. 410; *Kirkus Reviews*, September 1, 1979, p. 1036;
    Publishers Weekly, October 1, 1979, p. 80)

5. Brickman, Jennette, and George Haus. "*I Love Daddy or
    Role Development as a Function of Incestuous Behavior*."
    Arlington, Virginia: ERIC Document Reproduction Ser-
    vice, ED 143 181, 1978. 16 pp.

    Suggests that father-daughter incest can be considered
    a "family maintenance device." The willingness of a
    daughter to participate in such an incestuous relationship
    is considered a possible normal extension of female sex-
    role development. Examples of specific subcultures in
    Sweden, Japan, and the United States are used to demon-
    strate the contention that an incestuous family is
    actually an example of a "subculture."

6. Brooks, Barbara. "Families in Treatment for Incest."
    Ph.D. dissertation, University of Massachusetts, 1981.
    226 pp.

    Compares actual characteristics of incest families with
    stereotypes commonly presented in both popular and pro-
    fessional literature. Replies to questionnaires completed
    by members of families in treatment for incest contradicted
    many previous accepted opinions. For example, no evidence
    was found to support the belief that father-daughter
    incest occurs when the mother refuses the sexual advances
    of her husband. Similarly, no role reversals were evident
    between the mother and daughter in the cases studied.
    One common characteristic of the incest family was varying
    types of marital violence. Three areas of family dynamics
    were investigated: (1) family sexuality; (2) the marital
    relationship; and (3) parent-child interactions. (DAI
    XLII [1982])

7. Burgess, Ann Wolbert; A. Nicholas Groth; Lynda Lytle
    Holmstrom; and Suzanne M. Sgroi. *Sexual Assault of
    Children and Adolescents*. Lexington, Mass.: Heath,
    1978. 245 pp.

    Provides guidelines for assessment and management of
    sexual assault cases. Discussions of patterns of assault
    and techniques for comprehensive diagnosis and treatment
    are given. Each chapter is individually authored and
    deals with a specific area of childhood sexual assault.
    Although the book deals with childhood sexual assault in
    general, several chapters are either devoted to or use
    incest as part of their analysis. Specific topics dealing
    with incest include: (1) the problem of divided loyalties
    within the family structure when incest occurs and is
    reported; and (2) the coordination of community agencies
    in the treatment of incest. Community treatment is dis-
    cussed in a chapter by Henry Giarretto and concerns the
    work being done in Santa Clara County by the Child Sexual
    Abuse Treatment Program. Includes bibliography and index.
    (REVIEWS: *Contemporary Psychology*, January 1979, p. 49;
    Family Process, June 1979, pp. 215-218; *Social Work*,
    September 1979, p. 438)

8. Butler, Sandra. *Conspiracy of Silence: The Trauma of
    Incest*. San Francisco: New Glide, 1978. 208 pp.

    Focuses primarily on father-daughter incest and explores
    the dynamics of incest from the point of view of the
    victim, the mother, and the father. Personal testimonies

are included for each perspective. Includes the
following general observations on incest: (1) the
effect of incest can be serious and lasting; (2) research
on incest has been inappropriately focused on the lower
classes; (3) the closer the relation of the victimizer,
the less chance the incest will be reported; and (4)
there are inadequate social and community services to
deal with the problem. Concludes with personal comments
to family members and professionals. Includes notes and
bibliographies. (REVIEWS: *Booklist*, September 15, 1978,
p. 160; *Publishers Weekly*, March 6, 1978, p. 92)

9. Caruso, Michael F. "The Effects of Group Assertiveness
   Training on Assertiveness Dyadic Adjustment and
   Parenting Attitudes of Parents of Incestuous Families."
   Ph.D. dissertation, East Texas State University, 1980.
   242 pp.

   Investigated the overall effectiveness of including
   group assertiveness training in the treatment of members
   of incestuous families. Twelve male incest offenders
   and fifteen female spouses or non-marital partners of
   incest perpetrators were divided into two therapy groups:
   (1) a treatment group which involved various methods of
   teaching assertiveness and (2) a control group which was
   treated using conventional therapeutic approaches. Post-
   tests indicated no significant differences between the
   two groups with regards to assertiveness, dyadic adjust-
   ments, or parenting attitudes. Some nearly statistically
   significant differences were noted between male and female
   responses. (DAI XLI [1981])

10. Ciccone, Beverlee S. "The Development of an Instrument
    to Study Attitudes Towards Incest." Ph.D. dissertation,
    Temple University, 1982. 182 pp.

    Attempts to construct a reliable and valid instrument
    to measure attitudes toward incest with particular
    attention to measuring the attitudes of various types of
    health professionals. Describes how the instrument is
    validated and identifies the following groups for testing:
    individuals in medical school, nursing school, psychiatric
    residency, psychology doctoral programs, health education
    doctoral programs, marital and family training, and social
    work graduate programs. Measures differences in atti-
    tudes between these groups and also notes differences
    due to sex of the respondent. (DAI XLII [1982])

11. Connecticut State Department of Children and Youth
    Services. *An In-depth Look at X-Rated Problems in
    Families with Service Needs. Workshop Proceedings.*
    Arlington, Virginia: ERIC Document Reproduction
    Service, ED 179 857, 1979. 136 pp.

    Reproduces the proceedings of a series of four-day
    workshops conducted by the Deinstitutionalization of
    Status Offenders Project of the Department of Children
    and Youth Services and the Connecticut Justice for
    Children Collaboration during May 1979. Workshops dealt
    with the following issues of adolescent sexuality: (1)
    "Adolescent Sexuality--How Much Is Too Much?"; (2)
    "Incest--A Family Affair"; (3) "Prostitution--The Pros
    and The Conned"; and (4) "Adolescent Sexuality--Implica-
    tions for Program Development." The incest workshop
    describes various treatment programs and gives examples
    from Connecticut's Sexual Trauma Treatment Program.
    Sources of additional information are also listed.

12. Conte, Jan R. *A Child Welfare Perspective on Children's
    Versus Parent's Rights in Incestuous Families.*
    Arlington, Virginia: ERIC Document Reproduction Service,
    ED 194 855. 1980. 25 pp.

    Summarizes commonly accepted child and parents' rights
    and indicates the conflict which results in an incestu-
    ous family. Notes that, just as sexual abuse is a
    unique type of physical abuse, incest is a special case
    of child sexual abuse and must be treated in different
    ways. Intervention by social workers in cases of incest
    is a difficult decision and should be made in consulta-
    tion with representatives of the legal system.

13. Cooper, Karen Dendy. "Incest in Today's Society: An
    Orientation for Graduate Students in the Helping
    Professions." Ph.D. dissertation, University of
    South Carolina, 1979. 180 pp.

    Reports a study conducted to develop a program of
    incest education for graduate students entering human
    services professions. Informational content was deter-
    mined by sending questionnaires to educators, counselors,
    and treatment professionals. An instructional guide was
    developed and used in a two-day incest awareness work-
    shop. Evaluation of the workshop indicated that the
    intensive training on incest creates significant in-
    creases in cognitive awareness. (DAI XXXX [1979])

14. Cory, Donald Webster, and Robert E.L. Masters. *Violation of Taboo: Incest in the Great Literature of the Past and Present.* New York: Julian, 1963. 422 pp.

    Attempts to present a literary perspective on the subject of incest through an anthology of works by noted writers. Begins with an introductory overview of the religious, anthropological, sociological, and literary views of incest, including a discussion of Freud, Sophocles, Herman Melville and Thomas Mann. Works by these authors are discussed, as well as works by Marquis de Sade, Dylan Thomas, Nathaniel Hawthorne and W. Somerset Maugham.

15. Courtois, Christine Ann. "Characteristics of a Volunteer Sample of Adult Women Who Experienced Incest in Childhood or Adolescence." Ph.D. dissertation, University of Maryland, 1979. 336 pp.

    Explores the demographic characteristics of incest victims and the effects of the incestuous relationships. Results include: (1) impact of incest is "highly subject or idiosyncratic"; (2) the younger the age of the incest victim, the more severe the long-term effects; (3) cross-generational incest may be more frequent than supposed; and (4) effect of incest is negative and no evidence for positive incest was found. Also notes that women are willing to discuss their incestuous experiences in a research situation. (DAI XL [1979])

16. Courtois, Christine Ann, and Deborah Watts. *Women Who Experienced Childhood Incest: Research Findings and Therapeutic Strategies.* Arlington, Virginia: ERIC Document Reproduction Service, ED 198 406, 1980. 31 pp.

    Reports a correlational study of women who had been involved in incestuous relationships as children. Statistical analyses of various ratings of the aftereffects of the incest are presented. Variables considered include duration, frequency, use of coercion, disclosed or undisclosed, age at onset, and treatment therapies. Suggestions are made to aid therapists in dealing with incest victims. Recommends more "controlled research" be conducted to evaluate the effects of incest on victims.

17. Curry, Edythe Virginia. "A Study of Changes in Self-
     Concept of Incestuous Fathers While Undergoing
     Therapy." Ph.D. dissertation, United States Interna-
     tional University, 1981. 92 pp.

     Investigates the relationship between incestuous
     fathers, self-concept, and response to treatment.
     Details an experiment using the Tennessee Self Concept
     Scale as a measure of the self-concept of twenty-four
     incestuous fathers involved in group therapy. Statis-
     tical differences were found between scores of the norm
     population and the pretest scores of the subjects. Sig-
     nificant decreases in levels of confidence among the
     subjects were also noted from pretest to posttest. Two
     explanations for these results are presented. The in-
     fluence of the group therapy process is considered.
     (DAI XLII [1981])

18. Durkheim, Emile. *Incest: The Nature and Origin of the
     Taboo.* New York: Lyle Stuart, 1963. 119 pp.

     Examines the underlying anthropological and socio-
     logical basis of the incest taboo and its predominance
     in almost all societies. Attempts to understand the
     taboo by tracing its existence to its cultural origins.
     Explores the development of primitive societies with
     special attention to the clan structure and social regu-
     lations controlling behavior. Notes that regulations
     which control relations between men and women form an
     important part of clan society and that these regulations
     deal with ritualistic taboos related to exogamy and
     menstruation. Observes that "the dispositions of our
     codes relative to marriage between relatives are linked
     to the exogamic practices by a continuous series of
     intermediaries, even as our current domestic structure
     is linked to that of the clan." Published with Albert
     Ellis's *The Origins and the Development of the Incest
     Taboo* (see also #19). (REVIEWS: *American Anthropologist*,
     December 1964, p. 1404; *American Sociological Review*,
     October 1964, p. 776)

19. Ellis, Albert. *The Origins and the Development of the
     Incest Taboo.* New York: Lyle Stuart, 1963. 51 pp.

     Explores the incest taboo by reviewing the basic
     theories on the origin of taboo by noted sociologists

and anthropologists. Takes as its focus a reexamination
of Emile Durkheim's contention that the taboo is grounded
in "man's fundamental tendency to be obsessive-compulsive,
religio-superstitious, and ritualistic." Begins with a
review of works by Sigmund Freud, Bronislaw Malinowski,
Edward Westmark, Claude Lévi-Strauss and others. Notes
that these individuals generally hold views counter to
Durkheim's theory. Argues, however, that current evidence
indicates a biological, as well as environmental, basis
for human behavior and that innate irrational characteristics of the human species may involve the totems and
taboos which Durkheim felt formed the basis of the incest
taboo. Published with Emile Durkheim's *Incest: The
Nature and Origin of the Taboo* (see also #18).

20.   Esposito, Paul Andrew. "Consensual Incest: Towards a
      Natural History of Self-Definition of Deviance."
      Ph.D. dissertation, New York University, 1981. 270 pp.

      Studies two types of consensual incest: brother-sister
and extended relationships, e.g., cousins or uncle-niece.
The voluntary aspect of involvement in these incestuous
situations was found to be significant. Major differences are noted between characteristics of these relationships and other types of incest, e.g., father-
daughter incest in which the father usually forces the
daughter to participate. Consensual incestutous relationships do not seem to cause as much conflict or re-
sentment and do not generally occur within disrupted
families. Reactions of the participants are further
analyzed with regard to "labeling theory." Older
siblings are best able to rationalize their behavior.
(DAI XLII [1982])

21.   Finkelhor, David. *Sexually Victimized Children.*
      Riverside, N.J.: Free Press, 1979. 228 pp.

      Uses information obtained in a survey of six New
England colleges and universities and discusses the many
aspects of the sexual abuse of children. A major focus
is on incestuous relations. Explores such issues as
(1) the types of experience involved (kinds of sexual
activity, age of partner, prevalence and duration of
activity); (2) the incestuous activity itself (definition,
incidence, father-daughter incest, sibling incest); (3)
sources of trauma (measuring trauma, age differences,
homosexual experiences); (4) social backgrounds of
victims; and (5) family background of victim. Concludes
that: (1) large numbers of boys and girls are sexually

victimized; (2) preadolescent children are most vulnerable; (3) victimizers are mostly men; (4) many of the
sexual experiences are perceived negatively; (5) 75% of
female victims know their older partners; (6) father-
daughter incest is most traumatic; (7) social isolation
increases the chances of victimization; and (8) age of
victimizers affects the degree of trauma. Includes
appendix with a sample survey, bibliography, and index.
(REVIEWS: *New York Times Book Review*, January 27, 1980,
p. 12; *Social Forces*, September 1980, p. 311; *Sociology:
Reviews of New Books*, March 1980, p. 73)

22. Forward, Susan, and Craig Buck. *Betrayal of Innocence:
Incest and its Devastation*. Los Angeles: J.P. Teacher,
1978. 198 pp.

    Discovers and analyzes a wide range of incestuous
relationships. Notes that over a million people have
been the victims of incest and that girls outnumber boys
7-1. Observes that incest develops usually in troubled
families and that each family member suffers. Emphasis
is on father-daughter incest with detailed analysis on
the daughter, father, and the mother as silent partner.
Other types of incest include mother-son, sibling,
grandfather-granddaughter, mother-daughter and father-
son incest. Reviews the legal problems in defining,
reporting, and dealing with the incest offender and
victim. Also remarks on the difficulties therapists
have dealing with incest victims. Includes index and
bibliography. (REVIEWS: *British Journal of Psychiatry*,
February 1982, p. 221; *Kirkus Reviews*, July 1, 1978,
p. 776; *Library Journal*, October 15, 1978, p. 2119)

23. Fowler, John Howard. "The Development of Incest Regulations in the Early Middle Ages: Family, Nurturance,
and Aggression in the Making of the Medieval West."
Ph.D. dissertation, Rice University, 1981. 212 pp.

    Studies the development and extent of the incest taboo
in late Roman and early medieval societies. Various
theories concerning the incest ban are examined and a
possible synthesis presented. Finds a "causal connection
between the level of incest awareness in a society or in
individuals and the levels of intrasocietal or individual
aggression." Examples from different societies are given
to justify this hypothesis. Various cognitive and
functional applications of the incest taboo are also
considered. (DAI XLII [1981])

24. Fox, Robin. *The Red Lamp of Incest*. New York: Dutton, 1980. 271 pp.

    Presents an anthropological examination of the incest taboo. Contends that the book is a rewriting of Freud's *Totem and Taboo* "with a half a century of hindsight." Reviews research on primates, as well as the concepts of Freud and Lévi-Strauss. Argues that our species abhors incest and promotes exogamy not because of the consequences and not because we rationally conclude it is wrong but because we are the product of an evolution which finds incest unhelpful to sexual selection. The incest taboo is grounded in the survival mechanisms that maintain the species. Extrapolates this theory to contemporary issues including feminism, the family, and teenage pregnancy. Includes bibliography and index. (REVIEWS: *Booklist*, December 15, 1980, p. 545; *Choice*, March 1981, p. 987; *Library Journal*, September 1, 1980, p. 1747; *Psychology Today*, December 1980, p. 126)

25. Fredlund, Eric Victor. "Shitari Yanomano Incestuous Marriage: A Study of the Use of Structural, Lineal, and Biological Criteria When Classifying Marriages." Ph.D. dissertation, Pennsylvania State University, 1982. 194 pp.

    Examines the marriage rules of the Shitari Yanomano through an analysis of how marriages are classified and how marriage rules relate to the concepts of incest and exogamy. Employs criteria based on lineage, exogamy, genealogy, and prescriptive bilateral cross-cousin marriage and divides marriages into "legitimate" and "incestuous." Compares this analysis to the application of Shitari Yanomano marriage rules and observes that such rules are sometimes violated for biological reasons. (DAI XLIII [1982])

26. Frederickson, Renee Marie. "Incest: Family Sexual Abuse and Its Relationship to Pathology, Sex Role Orientation, Attitudes Toward Women, and Authoritarianism." Ph.D. dissertation, University of Minnesota, 1981. 201 pp.

    Uses a variety of standardized personality tests to compile empirical information concerning male incest offenders and their wives. Clinical observations were also analyzed. Comparisons with control groups revealed the following characteristics of the incest group: (1) incest husbands had more prior marriages; (2) incest couples had more children and lower socioeconomic status;

and (3) incest offenders showed "greater evidence of
psychopathic deviancy, paranoia, and schizophrenia than
control males." Incestuous men were also found to be
less masculine and their wives correspondingly less
feminine. (DAI XLII [1981])

27. Geiser, Robert L. *Hidden Victims: The Sexual Abuse of
    Children*. Boston: Beacon, 1979. 191 pp.

    Covers the general topic of sexual abuse of children
    with some attention to the issue of incest specifically.
    Examines such areas as: (1) the definition of incest;
    (2) the incidence of incest; (3) myths about incest; (4)
    the types of victims; (5) father-daughter incest; and
    (6) brother-sister, brother-brother, mother-son, father-
    son, and mother-daughter incest. Major emphasis con-
    cerning incest is placed on father-daughter with special
    attention on the family dynamics which promote an in-
    cestuous environment. Explores the role of the mother
    in father-daughter incest and the general effects on the
    victims. Reviews issues to be considered in the treat-
    ment of father-daughter incest. Recommends individually
    counseling the family members first, leading to counsel-
    ing in special groups. Uses the Child Sexual Abuse
    Treatment Program in Santa Clara County, California as
    an example of good treatment. Includes index and bibli-
    ography. (REVIEWS: *Kirkus Reviews*, September 15, 1979,
    p. 1106; *Library Journal*, September 1, 1979, p. 1706;
    Publishers Weekly, August 13, 1979, p. 52)

28. Giarretto, Henry. "Integral Psychology and the Treat-
    ment of Father-Daughter Incest." Ph.D. dissertation,
    California Institute of Asian Studies, 1978. 291 pp.

    Discusses the use of integral psychology at the Child
    Abuse Treatment Program in Santa Clara County (CSATP),
    California. Argues that traditional ways of handling
    incest cases, e.g., incarceration and separation of
    family members, aggravates the problem. Views father-
    daughter incest as the failure of both the mother and
    father to have their own needs met. Community-based
    treatment is recommended. Notes that CSATP has been
    successful in keeping the children with the family and
    preventing recidivism. (DAI XLI [1980])

29. Gligor, Alyce Mapp. "Incest and Sexual Delinquency: A
     Comparative Analysis of Two Forms of Sexual Behavior
     in Minor Females." Ph.D. dissertation, Case Western
     Reserve University, 1966. 299 pp.

     Examines and compares two groups of females involved
     either in father-daugher incest or in delinquent sexual
     behavior. Results did not confirm previous findings
     concerning incestuous families as to family disorganiza-
     tion, occupational adjustment of the father, or insta-
     bility in the marriage. Incidence of alcoholism was
     found to be significant among mothers and fathers in
     incestuous households. Incestuous fathers were found
     to be generally younger, were on a lower occupational
     level, and were more erratic in work habits. (DAI
     XXVII [1967])

30. Goodwin, Jean M. *Sexual Abuse Incest Victims and Their
     Families.* Boston: J. Wright, 1982.

     Unavailable for inspection. No reviews.

31. Harrer, Margaret N. "Father-Daughter Incest: A Study
     of the Mother." Ph.D. dissertation, Indiana Univer-
     sity, 1980. 95 pp.

     Investigates the role of the mother in overt father-
     daughter incest. Various hypotheses concerning the
     mother's overall mental state and her social adjustment
     are evaluated. Replies to a questionnaire by twenty-
     eight women whose husbands had recently been involved in
     an incestuous relationship with their daughters were
     compared to responses from a similar control group.
     Mothers in the incest group admitted more depression and
     other psychological symptoms and significant differences
     were also found in family environment measures. Con-
     cludes that these results "tend to confirm many clinical
     speculations about the role of the mother in overt
     father-daughter incest dynamics." (DAI XLI [1981])

32. Herman, Judith Lewis. *Father-Daughter Incest.*
     Cambridge, Harvard University, 1981. 282 pp.

     Employs a feminist perspective and discusses the many
     aspects of incest. Among the areas covered are: (1)
     the incidence of incest; (2) harmful effects; (3) the
     issue of blame; (4) case studies of incest victims; (5)
     disclosing the incest; (6) the criminal justice system;
     (7) preventing sexual abuse; and (8) the foundations of

the incest taboo. Argues that an understanding of
incest requires an understanding of the patriarchal
power structure that makes the father all powerful and
the female child defenseless. This power structure has
similarly influenced psychological theory on incestuous
behavior and resulted in laws that inadequately protect
the female victim. Provides a state-by-state listing
of laws concerning incest including parallel statutes
on rape and other sexual crimes. Extensive bibliography
and index. (REVIEWS: *Atlantic Monthly*, October 1981,
p. 108; *Family Process*, June 1982, pp. 258-260; *Library
Journal*, September 15, 1981, p. 1740)

33. Hirschman, Lisa Nicole. "Incest and Seduction: A Com-
     parison of Two Client Groups." Ph.D. dissertation,
     Boston University School of Education, 1979. 203 pp.

     Analyzes interviews with therapists regarding adult
     female clients who had experienced incestuous or seduc-
     tive relationships with their fathers. Family dynamics,
     client dynamics, and therapy are discussed. Indicates
     that victims of incest tend to have strong, negative
     identities while seductive individuals tend to have a
     vacillating self-image. Concludes that the damage to
     incest victims is probably more profound. (DAI XXXX
     [1979])

34. Holder, Wayne M., ed. *Sexual Abuse of Children: Impli-
     cations for Treatment.* Englewood, Colorado: American
     Humane Association, 1980. 111 pp.

     Provides a general discussion of child sexual abuse
     with considerable emphasis on family sexual problems,
     most notably incest. Meant to serve as a guide for
     professionals involved in the treatment of sexually
     abused children. Reviews such areas as the following:
     (1) the nature and extent of sexual abuse (considerable
     demographic data presented); (2) a descriptive analysis
     of father-daughter incest; (3) false accusations of
     incest; (4) problems in the identification and treatment
     of incest; (5) problems in the assessment and referral
     of incestuous family members; and (6) psychological
     treatment of family members. Includes extensive bibli-
     ography.

35. Horstmann, Nancy M. *Family Therapy with the Incestuous Family*. Arlington, Virginia: ERIC Document Reproduction Service, ED 212 926, 1981. 20 pp.

Demonstrates how a "structural family therapy model" can be used to treat "both the incestuous family who has remained intact or one which is making an effort to be re-united after an incident of abuse." The role of the therapist in helping the family members deal with each other is discussed. Outlines the characteristics of a typical incest family and shows how structural family therapy can be used in treating both the victim and the other members of the family. Notes that legal restrictions often conflict with treatment options.

36. Hughes, Katherine Ann. "The Reported Incidence of Incest Among Runaway Female Adolescents." Ph.D. dissertation, California School of Professional Psychology, Berkeley, 1980. 125 pp.

Considers the incidence of incest reported by female adolescent runaways. Distinguishes between overt incestuous contact and covert incestuous contact. Differences are also noted between incestuous relationships with biological as opposed to nonbiological father figures. Results verified predictions that incest would be frequently reported by runaway female adolescents. Such incestuous contact, however, more typically occurred with a nonbiological father figure. Responses to a questionnaire were solicited from girls at two runaway shelters in California over a four-month period. (DAI XL [1981])

37. Justice, Blair, and Rita Justice. *The Broken Taboo: Sex in the Family*. New York: Human Sciences, 1979. 304 pp.

Argues that people are ignorant of the facts regarding incest and that the problem is of considerable magnitude. Explores the following areas: (1) definition of incest and the purposes of the incest taboo; (2) the type of person who commits incest; (3) the role of the mother in incestuous families including mother-son incest; (4) familial factors promoting an incestuous relationship; (5) cues that indicate the presence of incest; (6) consequences of incest; and (7) the treatment of incest. Recommends that incest needs to be demystified and desexualized. Contends that incest grows out of parental inabilities to manage their stress and deal with sexual

relationships. Recommends public efforts to improve
parenting and stress management skills, coupled with
better reporting laws and treatment programs. Includes
notes, bibliography and index. (REVIEWS: *Library Journal*,
July 1978, p. 1466; *Science Books and Films*, March 1980,
p. 193)

38. Kegan, Katherine Anne. "Attachment and Family Sexual
     Abuse: An Investigation of the Families of Origin and
     Social Histories of Mothers from Present Incest Fami-
     lies." Ph.D. dissertation, University of Minnesota,
     1981. 214 pp.

     Considers the relationship between attachment and
     family sexual abuse. The importance of the "families
     of origin" in determining parental behaviors and atti-
     tudes is stressed. This intergenerational factor was
     studied through structured interviews conducted with
     mothers in incestuous families and mothers in a control
     group. Four scales were used to compare responses.
     Significant differences were evident on the Attachment
     and Chaos scales, but differences on the Parentification
     and Mother scales were not statistically significant.
     Explanations of these and other supplemental findings
     are presented. (DAI XLII [1982])

39. Knudson, Doris Gonzalez. "Interpersonal Dynamics and
     Mothers' Involvement in Father-Daughter Incest in
     Puerto Rico." Ph.D. dissertation, Ohio State Univer-
     sity, 1981. 165 pp.

     Describes a study conducted to: (1) identify the
     father-mother-daughter relationship in incestuous fami-
     lies; (2) determine the typical circumstances of the
     sexual abuse; and (3) consider the role of the mother.
     Interviews with twenty-four mothers whose daughters had
     been involved in father-daughter incest were conducted
     and case studies developed. Families were found to be
     dysfunctional and to be from all educational, economic,
     and social levels. Fathers were frequently alcoholics
     and physically abusive of their wives. Stresses the
     need for more research and better intervention tech-
     niques. Subjects had received counseling at the Puerto
     Rican Rape Crisis Center between 1978 and 1980. (DAI
     XLII [1982])

40. Kroth, Jerome A. *Child Sexual Abuse: Analysis of a Family Therapy Approach.* Springfield, Ill.: Charles Thomas, 1979. 200 pp.

    Analyzes the Child Sexual Abuse Treatment Program of Santa Clara County (CSATP), California, developed by Henry Giarretto to provide humanistic treatment to sexual abuse victims. Discusses and evaluates the program in the following areas: (1) computerized intake system for child abuse cases; (2) impact of family therapy on intra-familial abuse; (3) judicial versus therapeutic approaches to treatment; and (4) the CSATP training program. Provides background information on Parents United, the humanistic treatment model, and administration of the program. Includes annotated source list of child sexual abuse agencies and organizations. Also includes appendix, bibliography and index.

41. Krupnick, Martin Ira. "A Survey of School Psychologists' Awareness of and Attitudes Toward Incest." Ph.D. dissertation, Rutgers University, 1981. 111 pp.

    Approaches the problem of incest from the point of view of the school psychologist. Examines the abilities of the psychologist to identify, report and treat incest victims, particularly as they relate to institutional policies established by the schools, availability of training about incest victims, and legal reporting re-quirements. Observes that many schools lacked a policy on reporting incest cases and that psychologists felt a strong need for training in this area so that prevention and treatment could be affected. Recommends additional training and further research. (DAI XXXXIII [1982])

42. Larson, Noel Ruth Weber. "An Analysis of the Effective-ness of a State-Sponsored Program Designed to Teach Intervention Skills in the Treatment of Family Sexual Abuse." Ph.D. dissertation, University of Minnesota, 1980. 377 pp.

    Evaluates a training program designed to be used in the treatment of incest. Experimental and control groups of subjects were given a knowledge test and an incest attitude scale. They also observed a simulated interview with an active incest family. Intensive training in family therapy, including both didactic and small group supervision models, was postulated to improve

the overall ability of therapists to deal with incest
and incest victims. Results showed that such training
had little effect on knowledge or skill levels, but significantly improved the professional attitudes and
tolerance of the therapists. (DAI XL [1981])

43. Larson, Noel Ruth Weber. *Family Sexual Abuse Training
    Program.* Arlington, Virginia: ERIC Document Reproduc-
    tion Service, ED 178 197, 1979. 12 pp.

    Describes an extensive training program developed by
    the University of Minnesota Medical School, Department
    of Family Practice and Community Health Program in Human
    Sexuality for human service professionals involved in
    the treating of family sexual abuse. Content and time
    frame of the training are summarized and objectives out-
    lined. Evaluations were also conducted and are reported.
    Stresses the need for such training to be interdiscipli-
    nary in focus.

44. Latimore, Frances Kristin Creager. "Incestuous Family
    Members' Perceptions of Father and Family Environment."
    Ph.D. dissertation, United States International Univer-
    sity, 1981. 144 pp.

    Examines whether particular personality traits can be
    identified which distinguish between incestuous and non-
    incestuous fathers and families. Two groups of families,
    of which thirty-seven were incestuous and thirty-five
    were normal and nonincestuous, were given various self-
    report questionnaires and the results compared. Signifi-
    cant differences were noted in the opinions expressed
    concerning hostility and social behavior. Specifically,
    incestuous fathers were considered more hostile towards
    their families and to be socially withdrawn. No differ-
    ences were noted in terms of dominant behavior. While
    incestuous families believe they are as ethical and
    moral as nonincestuous families, other personality
    traits apparently contribute to the overt incestuous
    behaviors exhibited. (DAI XLII [1981])

45. McNaron, Toni A. *Voices in the Night: Women Speaking
    About Incest.* Minneapolis: Cleis Press, 1982. 196 pp.

    Unavailable for inspection.

46. Maisch, Herbert. *Incest*. New York: Stein and Day,
     1972. 252 pp.

     Provides a general examination of the psychological
     and sociological aspects of incestuous families. Begins
     with a cultural analysis of the incest taboo and a his-
     torical survey and discussion of the laws on incest.
     Proceeds to a broad review on the sociology, psychology
     and psychopathology of incest dealing with a variety of
     incestuous relationships: father-daughter, stepfather-
     stepdaughter, father-son, mother-son, mother-daughter
     and grandfather-granddaughter. Among the author's con-
     clusions are: (1) the incest taboo has resisted histori-
     cal or anthropological explanation; (2) the laws on
     incest are inconsistent and reflect an uncertainty as
     to how to treat victims and perpetrators; (3) incest is
     often committed by otherwise normal individuals, but the
     family is usually disturbed; and (4) negative effects on
     the family are often greater after disclosure. Includes
     bibliography, index and glossary of terms. (REVIEWS:
     Kirkus Reviews, August 1, 1972, p. 912; *Library Journal*,
     October 15, 1972, p. 3322; *Publishers Weekly*, August 14,
     1972, p. 40)

47. Martin, James O. "A Psychological Investigation of
     Convicted Incest Offenders by Means of Two Projective
     Techniques." Ph.D. dissertation, Michigan State Uni-
     versity, 1958. 95 pp.

     Examines and compares the personality characteristics
     of convicted incest offenders with other prisoners.
     Notes that incest offenders tended to be older, had more
     children and had less contact with crime than the control
     group. Found that incest offenders registered greater
     reactions in the areas of oral eroticism, castration
     anxiety, and Oedipal intensity. Also found that the
     incest group registered higher in being disturbed in
     psychosexual areas. (DAI XXI [1960])

48. Masters, R.E.L. *Patterns of Incest: A Psycho-social
     Study Based on Clinical and Historical Data*. New
     York: Julian Press, 1963.

     Examines the basic tenets of the incest taboo and
     concludes that there are no justifiable reasons for
     maintaining it. Proposes that, since "demonstrable
     damage" results from the taboo, it is necessary to "re-
     move completely the prohibition: to eliminate the de-
     structive, superstition-grounded concept of incest."

Includes lengthy excerpts from earlier works on incest
which allegedly support this radical theory. Emphasizes
the harmful aspects of maintaining a strict incest prohibition and urges the repeal of all "superfluous incest
statutes." Argues that anyone studying the incest taboo
must note the "terrible ravages" it causes and concludes
that "the benefits resulting from the prohibition must
be enormous to justify those ravages."

49. Meiselman, Karin C. *A Historical Perspective on the
    Treatment of Incest.* Arlington, Virginia: ERIC Docu-
    ment Reproduction Service, ED 256 154, 1981. 11 pp.

    Presents an historical overview of the treatment of
incest. Freud's beliefs and his impact on traditional
psychotherapeutic treatment of incest victims are noted.
Characteristics of incestuous fathers and family structure were analyzed extensively in the 1950s and 1960s.
The women's movement and the child protection lobby
which became prominent in the 1970s are shown to have
greatly accelerated the study of incest. Therapeutic
treatment has generally dealt either with intervention
in a current incestuous situation or treatment of the
long-term effects on victims.

50. Meiselman, Karin C. *Incest: A Psychological Study of
    Causes and Effects with Treatment Recommendations.*
    San Francisco: Jossey-Bass, 1978. 366 pp.

    Notes that the purpose of the book is "to provide
mental and health professionals who may be encountering
occasional incest cases with the accumulated observations and hypothesis of numerous clinicians and researchers...." Among the topics covered are: (1) a
discussion of the anthropological and sociological ori
gin of the incest taboo; (2) the research problems in
dealing with the topic of incest; (3) the psychological
causes and effects of incest; (4) a detailed description
and analysis of father-daughter incest; and (5) homosexual, brother-sister, and mother-son incest. Makes
recommendations regarding the prevention and treatment
of incest. Urges increased knowledge among professionals
on incest, improved and supportive reactions on the part
of community agencies, and improvement in legal codes.
Includes bibliography and index. (REVIEWS: *Society*,
September 1979, p. 87; *Sociology and Social Research*,
January 1981, pp. 246-247)

51. Meiselman, Karin C., and Nancy Sheehy. *The Effects of Incest on Therapist Assessment of Female Clients.* Arlington, Virginia: ERIC Document Reproduction Services, ED 211 899, 1981. 13 pp.

    Reports the results of a questionnaire given to 124 psychotherapists to investigate their preconceptions and opinions concerning incest. The hypothesis that therapists would be "unduly influenced by the theory that incest is conducive to serious pathology" was not supported. However, responses did support the prediction that therapists "would attribute great importance to incest as a cause of the client's disturbance." Experimental methods and statistical results are briefly presented.

52. Mrazek, Patricia, and C. Henry Kempe, eds. *Sexually Abused Children and their Families.* New York: Pergamon, 1981. 271 pp.

    Explores in detail the general area of child sexual abuse with numerous chapters dealing with various aspects of incest. Book is divided into five major categories: (1) Definition and recognition; (2) Sexual child abuse and the law; (3) Psychodynamics and evaluation; (4) Treatment; and (5) Prognosis and Outcome. Sections dealing with incest specifically cover such topics as: (1) sociological, psychopathic and psychodynamic views of incest; (2) types of incestuous relationships; (3) investigative techniques; (4) intervention and treatment; and (5) analysis of the dysfunctional family. Includes extensive bibliographies, footnotes. Also includes author and subject index. (REVIEWS: *British Journal of Psychiatry*, May 1982, p. 539; *Choice*, March 1982, p. 956)

53. Muldoon, Linda, ed. *Incest: Confronting the Silent Crime.* Arlington, Virginia: ERIC Document Reproduction Service, ED 178 826, 1979. 103 pp.

    Provides an overview of societal attitudes toward incest and estimates the incidence of incest. Chapters deal with the following: (1) Identification of the Victim and the Family; (2) The Reporting Statute; (3) Information Gathering and Assessment; (4) Using the Judicial System; (5) Providing Services; and (6) Prevention of Sexual Abuse. Written for those involved in law, medicine, education, and social services.

54. Oliviera, Susan Lynne. "A Phenomenological Study of Six
    Incestuous Fathers with Abusive Childhoods." Ph.D.
    dissertation, Union for Experimenting Colleges and
    Universities, 1981. 220 pp.

    Studies the childhood and family backgrounds of
    fathers who subsequently participated in father-daughter
    incest. Researchers conducting interviews of the
    fathers applied an existential, phenomenological ap-
    proach. Findings include: (1) fathers demonstrated low
    self-esteem, lacked impulse control and were involved in
    uncommunicative marital relationships; (2) fathers had
    bad feelings toward their childhoods where abuse occurred
    and revealed a need for nurturance, approval, and warmth;
    and (3) fathers identified with their daughters and
    imagined that they were receiving the nurturance they
    had missed as children. Discusses treatment particularly
    from the perspective of humanistic psychology and psycho-
    synthesis. (DAI XLIII [1982])

55. Pelto, Vonda Loretta. "Male Incest Offenders and Non-
    offenders: A Comparison of Early Sexual History."
    Ph.D. dissertation, United States International Uni-
    versity, 1981. 110 pp.

    Compares the early childhood sexual experiences of
    incest offenders and nonoffenders. Argues that the
    intergenerational aspects of child sexual abuse have
    typically been overlooked. Responses to a self-reporting
    questionnaire by incest offenders currently in therapy
    and normal nonoffenders attending a trade school were
    analyzed and childhood sexual experiences compared using
    the following variables: (1) incidence of victimizations;
    (2) profile of sexual abuse; (3) perpetrator; (4) sex of
    perpetrator; and (5) observation of incestuous sexual
    abuse. As hypothesized, incest offenders had both a
    larger number and wider variety of childhood sexual
    experiences. They also suffered more emotional trauma
    in their childhoods and were more likely to have been
    exposed to incest. (DAI XLII [1981])

56. Phelan, Patricia Kay. "The Process of Incest: A Cultural
    Analysis." Ph.D. dissertation, Stanford University,
    1981. 332 pp.

    Presents a cultural analysis of incest in American
    society. Interviews with incestuous parents and counse-
    lors and participant observation of therapy sessions were
    used to develop an understanding of the general topic.

The humanistic and judicial aspects of the treatment
community are shown to conflict in many areas. The
effects on relationships and their opinions of the event
differ widely, primarily because of differences in the
relationships involved (e.g., father-daughter or step-
father-stepdaughter). (DAI XLII [1981])

57. Pittman, Steven Gary. "A Personality Profile of Pedo-
    philiac and Incestuous Child Molesters: A Comparative
    Study." Ph.D. dissertation, United States Internation-
    al University, 1981. 142 pp.

    Using the Minnesota Multiphasic Personality Inventory
    (MMPI), the author attempted to discover differences in
    the personalities of pedophiliacs and incest perpetra-
    tors, and to determine the usefulness of the MMPI in
    reclassifying the subjects. Results indicated greatest
    difference in the area of depression with modest differ-
    ences for the Frequency and Social Introversion scales.
    Concludes that discriminate analysis can be used to
    identify differences and can be employed as an accurate
    tool for classifying pedophiliacs and incest perpetrators.
    (DAI XLIII [1982])

58. Reisinger, Mercedes Concepcion. "Psychological Test
    Profiles of Latency Aged Female Incest Victims: A
    Comparative Study." Ph.D. dissertation, Brigham
    Young University, 1981. 66 pp.

    Studies four groups of young girls between the ages of
    six and twelve (incest victims, incest victim siblings,
    outpatients, and a control sample) to determine if any
    significant psychopathological differences could be
    determined. Thirty-seven dependent variables were de-
    veloped and compared. Responses were obtained from the
    Personality Inventory for Children, the Children's Sen-
    tence Completion Test, the Draw-a-Family, and the The-
    matic Apperception Test. Results were statistically
    analyzed and significant findings related to earlier
    research. (DAI XLII [1981])

59. Renvoizé, Jean. *Incest: A Family Pattern.* London:
    Routledge & Kegan Paul, 1982.

    Unavailable for inspection.

60. Ricks, Chip. *Carol's Story*. Wheaton, Illinois: Tyndale House, 1981. 202 pp.

    Presents the personal narrative of Carol, a victim of childhood incest. This true story recounts her family life, the incestuous relationship with her father, and the emotional and psychological problems she encountered both as a child and as an adult. Written to make others aware of the "ugly shadow" of incest and to demonstrate the importance of God in resolving such serious problems. No bibliography or index.

61. Rodolfa, Emil R., and Thomas E. Whalen. *Attitudes Toward the Expression of Incestuous Fantasies*. Arlington, Virginia: ERIC Document Reproduction Service, ED 174 879, 1978. 9 pp.

    Reports the results of a survey conducted to determine if normal, nonpsychotic individuals had incest fantasies and, if so, how they regarded the fantasies. Questionnaires were completed by three different groups: (1) therapists handling incest cases; (2) counselors not involved with incest clients; and (3) members of the general public. Statistical analyses identified significant differences among the groups. While all admitted to experiencing incest fantasies, therapists treating incest victims tended to fantasize more and have better feelings toward their fantasies. Concludes that "nonpsychotic, well-functioning people did experience incest fantasies."

62. Rofsky, Marvin. "Effects of Father-Daughter Incest on the Personality of Daughters." Ph.D. dissertation, United States International University, 1979. 99 pp.

    Examines the effect of father-daughter incest on the personality of the daughter. Administered the Minnesota Multiphasic Personality Inventory to twenty female victims of childhood incest. Results indicated elevations on the Schizophrenia and Psychopathic Deviate scales. Concludes that these elevations may indicate personality disorders in the victims. Observes that these findings are consistent with previous studies on incest. (DAI XXXX [1980])

63. Roth, Richard A. *Child Sexual Abuse: Incest, Assault, and Sexual Exploitation*. Arlington, Virginia: ERIC Document Reproduction Service, ED 168 248, 1979. 31 pp.

    Defines sexual abuse of children and estimates the extent of the problem in the United States. Notes that

incest "usually has far more complicated temporary and
long-term repercussions." Effects on the victim and
other family members are described. Suggestions for
both prevention and treatment are briefly discussed.
Includes a bibliography and descriptions of fifteen
child abuse programs.

64. Sandell, Sandra Dianne. "'A Very Poetic Circumstance':
     Incest and the English Literary Imagination, 1770-
     1830." Ph.D, dissertation, University of Minnesota,
     1981. 236 pp.

     Reviews numerous English works of the period and notes
     a particular emphasis on brother-sister relationships.
     These relationships are characterized by a mutual re-
     spect, appreciation, and equality. Among the works dis-
     cussed are Scott's *The Antiquary*, Shelley's *Laon and
     Cynthia* and *The Cenci*, and Byron's *Cain*. (DAI XLII
     [1982])

65. Sanford, Linda Tschirhart. *The Silent Children*. New
     York: Doubleday, 1980. 367 pp.

     Examines child sexual abuse with particular emphasis
     on teaching children about the type of people and situa-
     tions which may lead to sexual molestation. Discusses
     the role of the family in the proper socialization of
     the child and explores in-depth the family dynamics
     which create the conditions for incest. The psychology
     of offenders and tactics used to gain cooperation of the
     victims are reviewed. Concludes that sexual abuse of
     children is an extension of our social value of male
     dominance. Provides specific observations on mother-
     son, father-son, mother-daughter, extended family-child,
     and sibling incest. Includes notes. (REVIEWS: *Kirkus
     Reviews*, July 15, 1980, p. 969; *Library Journal*, October
     1, 1980, p. 2067; *Publishers Weekly*, July 11, 1980, p. 80)

66. Santiago, Luciano P.R. *The Children of Oedipus: Brother-
     Sister Incest in Psychiatry, Literature, History and
     Mythology*. Roslyn Heights, N.Y.: Libra, 1973. 191 pp.

     Attempts to understand the psychotherapeutic aspects
     of brother-sister incest and stresses the need to inte-
     grate the humanities (history and literature) with the
     sciences. This approach is referred to as "psycho-
     humanities." Reviews the prehistorical and historical
     accounts of incest and discusses Greek and Philippine
     mythology and Egyptian, Roman and Oriental history. Also

reviews literary aspects of incest with attention to Byron, Chateaubriand, Goethe, Wagner, Melville and Hawthorne. Provides a review of psychiatric literature with some specific case histories. Includes bibliography. (REVIEW: *Journal of the American Academy of Child Psychiatry*, Winter 1975, pp. 184-185)

67. Schultz, LeRoy G., ed. *The Sexual Victimization of Youth.* Springfield, Ill.: Charles Thomas, 1980. 432 pp.

Collection of articles by noted authorities on many aspects of child sexual abuse. A major emphasis is on incest, with articles by Judith Herman, Lisa Hirschman, Henry Giaretto and LeRoy G. Schultz. General topics covered include the legal control of sexual abuse, the treatment of the victim by the judicial system, the child sex industry, and the diagnosis and treatment of victims. Areas specifically devoted to incest include discussions of father-daughter incest, the effects of incest, and humanistic treatment therapy. Concludes with recommendations for policy making on child pornography. Includes extensive bibliography. (REVIEW: *Social Work*, July 1981, p. 353)

68. Segner, Leslie Louise. "Two Studies of the Incest Taboo: I. Sexual Activity of Mice (*Mus Musculus*) as a Function of Familiarity. II. A Cross-Cultural Investigation of the Correlates of Incest in Myth." Ph.D. dissertation, University of Texas at Austin, 1968. 61 pp.

Explores the incest taboo in two ways: (1) conducted a clinical experiment with mice which concluded that close proximity tends to limit sexual attraction; and (2) examined the incest myths of thirty-one cultures. Reports that cultures which recognized the biological consequences of incest in their myths also imposed social deterrents to consanguineous marriages. Notes that this knowledge of consequences may be, in part, responsible for the incest taboo. (DAI XXIX [1968])

69. Shepher, Joseph. "Self-Imposed Incest Avoidance and Exogamy in Second Generation Kibbutz Adults." Ph.D. dissertation, Rutgers University, The State University of New Jersey, 1971. 298 pp.

Examines the phenomenon in the kibbutzim that second-generation adults do not marry individuals who, as children, had been in the same peer group. Investigates the socialization process for children and discusses

the effects of group solidarity ideology on inter-peer-
group marriages. Explains the incest avoidance behavior
using imprinting theory. (DAI XXXII [1971])

70. Siegel, Ken. *Group Treatment for Adolescent Girls in
    Incestuous Families.* Arlington, Virginia: ERIC Docu-
    ment Reproduction Service, ED 200 841, 1980. 10 pp.

    Describes two therapy groups comprised of female
    adolescent incest victims. Backgrounds of the girls
    are briefly summarized and the extent of the therapy
    session noted. Stresses the need for "immediate refer-
    ral" of incest victims and their placement in therapy.
    Individual counseling should be conducted concurrently
    with group treatment. Emphasizes that "therapists must
    come to grips with their own feelings regarding incest
    as a phenomenon in human relations."

71. Simari, C. Georgia, and David Baskin. *Incest: No Longer
    a Family Affair.* Arlington, Virginia: ERIC Document
    Reproduction Service, ED 182 616, 1979. 22 pp.

    Reviews the literature of incest research which is
    concerned with the "developmental and environmental
    patterns of individuals and families who have experi-
    enced incestuous events." Notes that most statistics
    compiled relating to incest are "grossly inaccurate."
    General issues of incest prevention, detection, and
    treatment are summarized.

72. Smith, Paul Edgar. "The Incest Motif and the Question
    of the Decadence of English Drama, 1603-1632." Ph.D.
    dissertation, University of Pittsburgh, 1980. 517 pp.

    Discusses the use of the incest motif in Jacobean and
    Caroline drama. The plays of Massinger, Beaumont and
    Fletcher, Tourneur, Middleton, and Ford are individually
    discussed and then their handling of incest as a theme
    is compared. Contends that these plays cannot accurately
    be labeled "decadent." All of the playwrights examined
    exhibit similar attitudes toward incest, but differences
    in artistic presentations are noted. Concludes that
    labeling dramas or dramatists as "decadent" probably is
    more of a subjective determination of a reviewer than an
    objective appraisal. (DAI XLII [1981])

73. Stein, Robert. *Incest and Human Love: The Betrayal of the Soul in Psychotherapy*. Baltimore: Penguin Books, 1974. 200 pp.

   Applies a psychoanalytical approach and takes as the main theme "the incest taboo and its significance for the development of human love." Argues that instinct has not been given its proper place in the therapeutic setting. Examines the universal character of the incest taboo; the cultural and psychological significance of incest; the characteristics of masculine and feminine psychology; the importance of Eros in psychological development; and the nature of transference. Includes bibliography and index. (REVIEW: *Journal of Analytical Psychology*, 1975, pp. 237-238)

74. Strauss, Patricia Lawrence. "A Study of the Recurrence of Father-Daughter Incest Across Generations." Ph.D. dissertation, California School of Professional Psychology, 1981. 228 pp.

   Explores the phenomena of child incest victims who marry and become the mothers of daughters who also become incest victims. Thirty adult women who were victims of incest by their fathers as children were interviewed and tested. One-half of the subjects were mothers in families in which father-daughter incest had also occurred. In comparing the families where incest has reoccurred with the families where incest has not occurred, author notes: (1) significant functional and personality differences between the repeat and nonrepeat families; and (2) significant difference in the interactions and reactions from friends, spouses and therapists when the subjects were molested as children. Subjects who received nonblaming support developed healthy families of their own. (DAI XXXII [1982])

75. Tormes, Yvonne M. *Child Victims of Incest*. Denver: American Humane Association, 1968. 40 pp.

   Draws from a larger research study on protecting child victims of sex crimes. Focuses on the family members, particularly in their potential capacity to inhibit or encourage incestuous relationships. Notes that the only available agent to prevent incest is the mother who often exhibits passive personality traits and demonstrates reluctance to seek public assistance. Argues that the

goal of child protective services is to remove the incest
perpetrator from the home. Identifies symptoms evident
in families where incest is likely to occur. These
symptoms include: (1) limited contacts to the outside
world; (2) rigid control by the father; (3) alcoholic or
abusive behavior by the father; (4) early marriage of
long duration; and (5) a large family with many young
children. Includes references.

76. Traver, Harold Henry. "The Theory and Practice of
    Incest." Ph.D. dissertation, University of California,
    Santa Barbara, 1973. 402 pp.

    Examines the significance and place of the incest taboo
    in society. Obtains data on the public's attitude and
    authorities' attitudes to the discovery of incest. Ar-
    gues that the incest taboo is primarily a theoretical
    construct required by general concepts of social order
    and the family's place in maintaining that order. This
    is contrasted with the view that there are empirical
    grounds for the taboo. (DAI XXXIV [1974])

77. Watts, Deborah L. *Psychological Intervention in Cases
    of Incest: Treatment Issues.* Arlington, Virginia:
    ERIC Document Reproduction Service, ED 159 516, 1979.
    12 pp.

    Describes various therapeutic approaches to dealing
    with incest victims. Briefly summarizes victim charac-
    teristics, general counseling considerations, and group
    therapy for all family members. Four areas of trauma to
    the victim are analyzed: (1) social; (2) emotional; (3)
    physical; and (4) sexual. Case studies are also pre-
    sented. Urges a "more humanistic and open approach to
    dealing with what has long been considered a dark and
    painful secret."

78. Weinberg, Samuel Kirson. *Incest Behavior.* Secaucus,
    N.J.: Citadel, 1955. 291 pp.

    Considered one of the first book-length studies of
    incest. Views the study of incest in the broader context
    of personality development, family relationships and
    social organization. Begins with an anthropological and
    historical examination of the incest taboo and subse-
    quently examines numerous cases of incest. The cases
    include father-daughter, brother-sister, mother-son, and
    combinations of father-daughter and brother-sister in-
    cest. Effects on the family both before and after
    detection of the incest are noted. The social setting

and personality development of the participants are examined. Concludes that incestuous behavior confuses family roles: in father-daughter incest, the family is characterized by paternal dominance; in sibling incest, the father does not dominate the family; in mother-son incest, maternal dominance is present. Argues that the incest taboo is essential to personality development, family integration and social cohesion.

79. Woodbury, J., and E. Schwartz. *The Silent Sin: A Case History of Incest*. New York: American Library, 1971.

Presents an allegedly true case study of father-daughter incest from the perspective of the victim. Acknowledges that the content may be "shocking and crude on occasion." Eleven visits to the therapist over a three-month period are recounted in great detail. Little factual material concerning incest and its treatment is present. Written for the popular audience. (REVIEW: *Journal of Sex Research*, May 1975, pp. 174-175)

II

PSYCHOLOGICAL ARTICLES

80. Arndt, William B., and Barbara Ladd. "Sibling Incest
    Aversion as an Index of Oedipal Conflict." *Journal
    of Personality Assessment* 45 (February 1981): 52-58.

    Explores the possibility of using sibling incest aver-
    sion as an index of the Oepidal complex. Ninety students
    were asked to respond to a series of one hundred ques-
    tions on brother-sister incest. Their responses were
    correlated with their guilt disposition, neuroticism,
    extraversion, and sensitization-repression. Findings in-
    clude: (1) males with sisters had a higher aversion to
    incest; (2) low-aversion females tended to express guilt-
    free attitudes toward sex; (3) middle-aversion females
    tended to have high sex guilt and display greater neuroti-
    cism. Concludes that sibling incest aversion may be a
    valid index for the Oedipal complex.

81. Awad, George A. "Single Case Study: Father-Son Incest--
    A Case Report." *Journal of Nervous and Mental Disease*
    162 (February 1976): 135-139.

    Reviews the literature on the incidence of father-
    daughter, brother-sister and homosexual incest. Examines
    a case of father-son incest occuring three times in a
    period of six weeks. Family history is reviewed with
    particular attention focused on the father who committed
    incestuous acts under the influence of alcohol. The
    mother exhibits denial. Reports that treatment centered
    on the father because the problem dealt primarily with
    his "intrapsychic" difficulties. Treatment involved
    eight sessions of joint marital therapy with positive
    results. Father was reported to be struggling with homo-
    sexual impulses on the unconscious level. Points out
    that this incest case is somewhat different from cases
    involving father-daughter incest.

33

82. Becker, Judith V.; Linda J. Skinner; Gene G. Abel; and
    Eileen C. Treacy. "Incidence and Types of Sexual
    Disfunctions in Rape and Incest Victims." *Journal of
    Sex and Marital Therapy* 8 (Spring 1982): 65-74.

    Reports the results of a study conducted to determine
    the frequency of sexual dysfunctions in female incest
    and rape victims. Subjects provided detailed sexual
    histories and took the Sexual Arousal Inventory. Chronic
    sexual dysfunctions, including sexual fears and loss of
    arousal or desire, were found to be "relatively common
    in rape and incest victims." Significantly, these dys-
    functions remain long after the sexual abuse.

83. Berest, Joseph J. "Medico-Legal Aspects of Incest."
    Journal of Sex Research 4 (August 1968): 195-205.

    Provides legal and medical definitions of incest.
    Notes that individuals who initiate incest are psychi-
    atrically abnormal, exhibiting such traits as neurosis,
    alcoholism, psychosis or paranoia. Observes that daugh-
    ters who are victims of incest may become promiscuous or
    suicidal. Several case histories with sample interviews
    from victims are presented.

84. Berry, Gail W. "Incest: Some Clinical Variations on a
    Classical Theme." *Journal of the American Academy of
    Psychoanalysis* 3 (April 1975): 151-161.

    Studies four aspects of incest: (1) brother-sister
    incest; (2) incest as a transferable characteristic; (3)
    homosexual incest; and (4) incest envy. Argues that in-
    cest is much more common than reported in psychoanalytic
    research. The aggressive nature of incest and the possi-
    bility of identifying "incest carriers" are noted. The
    psychiatric nature of the act of incest is also discussed
    in some detail. Seven case studies are included.

85. Boekelheide, Priscilla Day. "Sexual Adjustment of College
    Women Who Experience Incestuous Relationships." *Journal
    of the American College Health Association* 26 (June
    1978): 327-330.

    Examines the immediate and long-term effects of incest
    on female victims. Six case studies involving college
    women who had been involved in incestuous relationships
    are reported. Notes that the reactions can involve both
    antisocial and neurotic behavior. The need for effective
    psychotherapy is stressed. Effects on the victim's emo-
    tional adjustment and adult sex life are also noted.

86. Brown, Selma. "Clinical Illustrations of the Sexual
    Misuse of Girls." *Child Welfare* 58 (July-August 1979):
    435-452.

    Examines various cases of female victims of childhood
    incest, with particular attention to the effects of the
    incest in childhood. Notes that the most commonly re-
    ported incest is father-daughter and that onset usually
    begins between the ages of eight and nine. Effects of
    incest on the child include "poor self-esteem; a tendency
    to be masochistic in their relationships, particularly
    with males; a poor female sexual identity; and no ability
    to tolerate the frustration that intellectual learning
    demands." Concludes that incest is definitely harmful.

87. Browning, Diane H., and Bonny Boatman. "Incest: Children
    at Risk." *American Journal of Psychiatry* 134 (January
    1977): 69-72.

    Reviews fourteen cases of incest treated at the Child
    Psychiatry Clinic at the University of Oregon. Cases
    were divided into three categories: (1) father-daughter
    incest; (2) incest with uncle; and (3) multiple incest.
    Treatments and outcomes are briefly described. Found
    that families tended to have a chronically depressed
    mother, an alcoholic and/or violent father or male rela-
    tive, and an eldest daughter who, in assuming many of
    her mother's responsibilities, became involved in an
    incestuous relationship.

88. Burgess, Ann Wolbert, and Lynda Lytle Holmstrom. "Sexual
    Trauma of Children and Adolescents: Pressure, Sex, and
    Secrecy." *Nursing Clinics of North America* 10
    (September 1975): 551-563.

    Reviews cases of incest and other forms of sexual
    abuse reported at the Victim Counseling Program at Boston
    City Hospital. Examines various aspects of sexual abuse
    including: (1) relationship of offender to victim; (2)
    pressuring of victims into sexual activity; (3) types of
    sexual activity and reactions; (4) keeping secret and
    disclosing the secret acts; and (5) clinical treatment
    of the victim.

89. Cantwell, H.B. "Sexual Abuse of Children in Denver 1979:
    Reviewed with Implications for Pediatric Intervention
    and Possible Prevention." *Child Abuse and Neglect* 5
    (1981): 75-85.

    Analyzes 287 cases of child sexual abuse investigated
    by the Denver Department of Social Services in 1979.

Statistics are given and recommendations for improving
interview techniques with both victims and offenders are
summarized. Father-daughter or parent-surrogate perpetrators were involved in over half of the reported cases.
Most victims were under twelve and in some cases the incestuous relationship had extended over seven years.
Methods of intervention and prevention are also considered.

90. Cavallin, Hector. "Incestuous Fathers: A Clinical
    Report." *American Journal of Psychiatry* 122 (April
    1966): 1132-1138.

    Reviews a psychiatric study of 381 convicted felons at
    Kansas State Reception and Diagnostic Center. Analyzes
    twelve cases in which the convicts participated in
    father-daughter incest. Among the findings are: (1)
    incestuous fathers seldom had previous convictions or a
    history of mental illness or alcoholism; (2) incestuous
    fathers generally were married only once and possessed
    large families; (3) wives were perceived by the fathers
    as rejecting and threatening; (4) fathers exhibited
    projecting or paranoid thinking; and (5) fathers exhib-
    ited weak psychosocial identity, weak object relations
    and unconscious homosexual striving. Argues that con-
    victs' hostility toward their mothers was reactivated
    in the marital and family environment. The incest was
    "an expression of unconscious hostility that fuses with
    primitive genital impulses and is discharged toward the
    daughter."

91. Cohen, Jonathan A. "Theories of Narcissism and Trauma."
    American Journal of Psychotherapy 35 (January 1981):
    93-100.

    Examines a case of father-daughter incest in order to
    demonstrate that "self-pathology is a structural conse-
    quence of psychic trauma." Offers an organizational
    approach to psychopathology and argues that psychic
    trauma interferes with the normal development of memory
    and affects. Contends that the more severe the pathology
    the greater the possibility it is based on real traumas
    which must be transformed into normal memories and
    affects.

92. Cohen, Tamar. "The Incestuous Family." *Social Casework*
    62 (October 1981): 494-497.

    Discusses some of the current viewpoints on the in-
    cestuous family. Topics covered include the incidence

of father-daughter, brother-sister, and mother-son incest; psychological effects on incest victims; dynamics of the classical incestuous family; and therapeutic approaches. Notes that many incest victims reveal their past incestuous contact early in therapy and that the therapist should react empathetically so that the clients can express their guilt and confusion. Observes that families in which incest occurs may be searching in their own way for warmth, comfort, and nurturance.

93. Connell, H.M. "The Wider Spectrum of Child Abuse." *Medical Journal of Australia* 2 (October 7, 1978): 391-392.

Suggests that more attention must be given to sexual child abuse. Nine cases of various types of sexually assaulted children treated in a children's hospital are analyzed. Age of the victim, relationship of the perpetrator, duration of the relationship, medical complaints, and method of discovery are summarized for each case. Notes that "the strong taboos which surround this subject and likely legal involvement cause some doctors to shun these cases."

94. Conran, Michael B. "Incestuous Failures: Studies of Transference Phenomena with Young Psychotic Patients and Their Mothers." *International Journal of Psycho-Analysis* 57 (November 1976): 477-481.

Explores the dynamics of the schizophrenic patient by concentrating on the psychology of the mother while the patient was pre-adolescent. Notes that the families of schizophrenics often possess three features: (1) a symbiotic tie between mother and child in which the mother depends on the child to understand her feelings; (2) a father deficient in the parental and masculine role; and (3) confused communication based upon the conflicting wishes and needs of mother and child. Argues that the schizophrenic condition is based on incestuous failure, "which is failure of that early incestuous relationship which is part of early normal attachment experience; and which makes later incestuous acts or anxiety in adolescence necessary."

95. Cormier, Bruno M., and Paul Boulanger. "Life Cycle and Episodic Recidivism." *Canadian Psychiatric Association Journal* 18 (August 1973): 283-288.

Reports on a study involving two incestuous families which investigated episodic recidivism and recurrent

psychopathological states. Both cases involved isolated
incidents of incest over a period of many years. Case
histories and treatments are described. The effect of
the incestuous behavior on other members of the family
and the dominance of the wife in both cases are noted.
Stresses that studies which consider both the psycho-
social and psychosexual aspects of the problem are best
when dealing with incest.

96. Courtois, Christine Ann, and Deborah L. Watts. "Counsel-
    ing Adult Women Who Experienced Incest in Childhood or
    Adolescence." *Personnel and Guidance Journal* 60
    (January 1982): 275-279.

    Provides a discussion for the counselor on key aspects
    in the treatment of incest victims. Notes that the adult
    client may be reluctant to reveal childhood incest and
    that the counselor must attempt to get the information
    in a calm and straightforward fashion. Recommends that
    following an incestuous disclosure, counselor should
    find out the duration of the incestuous activity, age of
    onset, frequency, identity of the perpetrator, whether
    force was used, whether other family members knew about
    it, and whether the act was consensual or nonconsensual.
    Advises counselors to be patient and understanding.
    Discusses various treatment approaches.

97. Delson, N., and M. Clark. "Group Therapy with Sexually
    Molested Children." *Child Welfare* 60 (March 1981):
    175-182.

    Describes a play therapy group involving victims of
    sexual abuse who were under twelve years of age developed
    by the Humboldt County (California) Child Sexual Abuse
    Treatment Program. The design and structure of the model
    play therapy group is presented and the therapeutic
    techniques used are identified. Aim of the therapy is
    to enhance the victim's self-respect. Group and indi-
    vidual therapy for all family members, especially if
    incest is involved, are also available and highly recom-
    mended.

98. Dixon, Katherine N.; Eugene L. Arnold; and Kennth Cales-
    tro. "Father-Son Incest: Underreported Psychiatric
    Problems." *American Journal of Psychiatry* 135 (July
    1978): 835-838.

    Reports six case studies of father-son incest. Most
    victims were the oldest child and the fathers typically

had histories of alcoholism, sociopathy or violence.
Suggests that the sex of the parent involved in an incestuous relationship is a more important variable than
the sex of the child. Concludes that the frequency of
father-son incest is much higher than normally reported
or assumed by psychotherapists. Disclosure of the incest generally resulted in at least one person, usually
the father or the son, being separated from the rest of
the family.

99. Eist, Harold I., and Adeline U. Mandel. "Family Treat-
    ment of Ongoing Incest Behavior." *Family Process* 7
    (September 1968): 216-232.

    Presents a lengthy description of the ongoing therapy
    of a family involved in a variety of unusual sexual
    behaviors. The family consisted of the parents and six
    children, all of whom either participated in or observed
    intrafamilial sexual activities. Incest was a significant
    component of the family's sexual life. Therapeutic
    techniques are described in some detail. Advantages of
    having a male and a female working together as cothera-
    pists is emphasized.

100. Forseth, L.B., and A. Brown. "A Survey of Intrafamilial
     Sexual Abuse Treatment Centers: Implications for In-
     tervention." *Child Abuse and Neglect* 5 (1981):
     177-186.

     Reports the results of a survey conducted of treatment
     programs to determine what methods were being used to
     counsel and treat incestuous families. Group therapy
     was overwhelmingly recommended, but in many cases not
     as readily available. Treatment on an outpatient basis
     using an interdisciplinary staff approach was most
     frequently reported. The need for legal involvement
     and required family therapy was also noted. Includes
     many references.

101. Garrett, Thomas B., and Richard Wright. "Wives of
     Rapists and Incest Offenders." *Journal of Sex Re-
     search* 11 (May 1975): 149-157.

     Summarizes interviews conducted with eighteen wives
     of rapists and incest offenders at Atascadero State
     Hospital. Purpose was to study how the wives handled
     the "psychic burden" of having husbands who were com-
     mitted to hospital for sex offenses. Notes that (1)
     the wives were generally on a higher educational level

than their husbands; (2) the wives derived satisfaction
as martyrs; (3) the wives were surprised by their husbands' anti-social behavior; and (4) the wives felt
their marriages had not suffered. Authors conclude
that wives may use the behavior of their husbands to
reinforce the wives' social and moral dominance.

102. Giaretto, Henry. "Humanistic Treatment of Father-Daugh-
      ter Incest." *Journal of Humanistic Psychology* 18
      (Fall 1978): 59-76.

      Reviews a typical case of father-daughter incest and dis-
      cusses how the Child Sexual Abuse Treatment Program (CSATP)
      of Santa Clara County, California, deals with the situa-
      tion. Reports on the prevalence and impact of incest
      based on the CSATP experience, and describes the found-
      ing and humanistic approach of this treatment program.
      The fundamental principles and methods of the program
      are noted and preliminary results are discussed. Among
      the principles mentioned are (1) the family is viewed
      as an organic system; (2) the marital relationship is
      treated as a key factor; (3) high self-concept is neces-
      sary for healthy families; and (4) low self-concept may
      stimulate hostile and destructive behavior. Concludes
      that current attitudes and laws are ill-conceived and
      that the humanistic approach is best for troubled fami-
      lies.

103. Giaretto, Henry. "The Treatment of Father-Daughter
      Incest: A Psycho-Social Approach." *Children Today* 5
      (July-August 1976): 2.

      Reviews the history, purpose and effectiveness of the
      Child Sexual Abuse Treatment Program in Santa Clara
      County, California. Identifies the program objectives.
      These include: (1) providing immediate counseling and
      assistance to victims and other family members; (2)
      reconstructing the family and marriage; and (3) co-
      ordinating social services to assist the family. Notes
      the development of two related groups, Parents United
      and Daughters United, formed to share common experiences
      of family members involved in incest. Indicates that
      by using a treatment model based on humanistic psycholo-
      gy, children are returned to families sooner, marriages
      are preserved and recidivism is prevented.

104. Goodwin, Jean M., and Peter DiVasto. "Mother-Daughter Incest." *Child Abuse and Neglect* 3 (1979): 953-957.

   Presents a case study of mother-daughter incest. Similarities with father-daughter incest are noted. Therapists must be more aware of the possibility of mother-daughter incest because it is undoubtedly "more common than the rare case reports would indicate." Suggestions to aid in the detection of mother-daughter incest are presented. Predicts that reports of such incest may become more common as more female homosexuals serve as single parents of daughters.

105. Goodwin, Jean M.; Mary Simms; and Robert Bergman. "Hysterical Seizures; A Sequel to Incest." *American Journal of Orthopsychiatry* 49 (October 1979): 690 703.

   Reports six cases of hysterical seizures which developed after incest and were relieved after appropriate psychotherapy. Suggests that as many as ten percent of hysterical seizure cases seen by therapists may be directly related to earlier incestuous activity. Notes that "hysteroepilepsy might be a particularly natural symptom choice for incest victims" and relates this theory to early Navajo and Greek beliefs about incest and epilepsy.

106. Goodwin, Jean M.; T. McCarthy; and P. DiVasto. "Prior Incest in Mothers of Abused Children." *Child Abuse and Neglect* 5 (1981): 87-95.

   Reports the results of a study to determine if mothers of abused children had higher incidences of incest. Compared to a similar control group, mothers of abused children did report a significantly higher number of prior incestuous activities, twenty-four percent as opposed to only three percent for the control group. Similarly, fewer of the victimized mothers of abused children had been able to report the incest. Two case studies are presented and references are included.

107. Green, C.M. "Filicidal Impulses as an Anniversary Reaction to Childhood Incest." *American Journal of Psychotherapy* 36 (April 1982): 264-271.

   Describes a case of "maternal filicidal impulse" which resulted from the mother's childhood incestuous experiences. Two and a half years of intensive psychotherapy

are summarized. The psychodynamics of filicide are
briefly noted. The case study presented involves an
"anniversary reaction," i.e., the overt symptoms of the
mother coincided with her daughter reaching the age at
which the mother had been involved in an incestuous
experience.

108. Gross, Meir. "Incestuous Rape: A Cause for Hysterical
      Seizures in Four Adolescent Girls." *American Journal
      of Orthopsychiatry* 49 (October 1979): 704-708.

      Presents four cases of father-daughter incest which
      resulted in hysterical seizures by the adolescent vic-
      tims. Clinical identification of incest is difficult,
      but these cases emphasize the necessity of taking a
      detailed family history of all females referred to a
      therapist for treatment of hysterical seizures. Simi-
      larities among the cases, e.g., all offenders were
      alcoholics and had initially raped their daughters, are
      noted.

109. Gruber, Kenneth J. "The Child Victim's Role in Sexual
      Assault by Adults." *Child Welfare* 60 (May 1981):
      305-311.

      Investigates the various factors which must be con-
      sidered when a child accuses an adult of improper sexual
      activity. Both emotional and situational variables are
      identified. The entire procedure is further complicated
      when incest is suspected. Admonishes therapists to be
      aware of the consequences of blaming the victim for the
      sexual activity.

110. Gutheil, Thomas G., and Nicholas C. Avery. "Multiple
      Overt Incest as Family Defense Against Loss." *Family
      Process* 16 (March 1977): 105-116.

      Presents a detailed case study of father-daughter in-
      cest that involves both multiple incest with various
      daughters and intensive family therapy. Family members
      are described and the history of the incestuous rela-
      tionships outlined. Notes that incest was used in this
      instance as a "defense against the pain of separation."
      Separation or dissolution of the family was an extreme
      "preoccupation" of all family members and may have
      contributed to the overt incestuous behavior. This
      particular case study is related to other reported
      incidences of incest and a lengthy bibliography is
      included.

111. Harbert, Terry L.; Michel Hersen; David H. Barlow; and
     James B. Austin. "Measurement and Modification of
     Incestuous Behavior: A Case Study." *Psychological
     Reports* 34 (February 1974): 79-86.

     Concerns the treatment of a case of incest using
     behavior modification techniques. A fifty-two-year-old
     male who had committed repeated incestuous acts with
     his daughter was subjected to covert sensitization, an
     aversive technique. Reviews patient's sexual history
     and discusses the objective and subjective measures
     employed. Audiotapes and slides were employed as part
     of the covert sensitization. Contends that incestuous
     behavior, like other sexually deviant behavior, can be
     modified using covert sensitization without adversely
     affecting the other healthy aspects of the father-
     daughter relationship.

112. "Help for Families Coping with Incest." *Practice
     Digest* 1 (September 1978): 19-22.

     Describes the activities of the Boulder County Sexual
     Abuse Mini Team which provides short-term crisis coun-
     seling for families in which incest or sexual assault
     has occurred. Discusses the techniques used in inter-
     viewing both the parents and the child. Of particular
     importance is the interview with the father and the
     level of denial exhibited. Reviews the techniques of
     short-term treatment for all family members and dis-
     cusses results of the program to date.

113. James, Jennifer, and Jane Meyerding. "Early Sexual
     Experience as a Factor in Prostitution." *Archives
     of Sexual Behavior* 7 (January 1978): 31-42.

     Compares the early sexual experiences of prostitutes
     and nonprostitute women. Prostitutes were found to
     have experienced more sexual advances by elders, were
     more victimized by incest, typically began sexual
     activity earlier, and experienced a higher incidence of
     rape as children. Concentrates on incest and rape as
     "abusive sexual experiences" which can influence the
     development of atypical adult sexual activity.

114. James, Kathleen Lehigh. "Incest: The Teenager's
     Perspective." *Psychotherapy: Theory, Research and
     Practice* 14 (Summer 1977): 146-155.

     Proclaims that the purpose of the article is "to in-
     form about the teenage woman's experience and perception

of incest and ... report on one form of treatment used
to help these young women cope with and adjust to societal and family reaction to them as incest victims."
Studies seven teenagers committed to a juvenile institu-
tion. Employing a group therapy technique participants
revealed that the incestuous acts themselves were not
as damaging as the trauma they experienced when the
incest was revealed. Blame, rejection, and scapegoating
occurred within the family and counselors paid too much
attention to the act itself rather than letting the
victim talk about her feelings. Recommends that incest
be decriminalized and that perpetrators be given a
treatment sentence. Also recommends greater use of
existing agencies and greater education of professionals
and lay people in dealing with this problem.

115.   Johnston, Mary S. Krentz. "The Sexually Mistreated
       Child: Diagnostic Evaluation." *Child Abuse and
       Neglect* 3 (1979): 943-951.

       Examines the case of ten children who were abused
either by family members or individuals close to the
family. Children were given the Conger Sentence Comple-
tion Test, the Kinetic Family Drawing Test, and the
Conner Children's Self-rating Scale. Results indicated:
(1) children demonstrated a need for nurturance; (2)
children felt insecure and unsafe; (3) the family of
the children was disturbed in terms of roles and relationships; (4) children exhibited depression and sleep
disturbances; and (5) no differences could be found in
effects between children victimized by family and non-
family members. Recommends that treatment focus on the
dysfunctional family.

116.   Jorne, Paula Slager. "Treating Sexually Abused Chil-
       dren." *Child Abuse and Neglect* 3 (1979): 285-290.

       Discusses the treatment and characteristics of fami-
lies involved in the sexual abuse of children. Notes
that in cases of incest the child may feel very guilty,
particularly if the disclosure of incest breaks the
family apart. The mother is viewed as a central figure
exhibiting symptoms of depression and withdrawal, al-
lowing the child to serve as the sexual object for the
husband. Observes that abused infants may have sleep
or eating disorders and that abused adolescents may
exhibit sexually aggressive behavior, wear seductive
clothing, or be promiscuous or delinquent. Recommends

that treatment recognize incest as a family stress problem and that individual therapy for the child and group therapy for the parents are useful treatment approaches.

117. Kaslow, F.; D. Haupt; A.A. Arce; and J. Werblowsky. "Homosexual Incest." *Psychiatric Quarterly* 53 (Fall 1981): 184-193.

   Observes that there is a dearth of cases reported on homosexual incest in the literature. Provides two case studies of sibling homosexual incest and analyzes the psychodynamics of the patients. Notes that these incest victims may exhibit severe psychopathology including suicidal behavior. Recommends a treatment which includes sessions with "members of the family of origin as well as several sessions with the family of procreation." Contends that the effects of homosexual incest are considerable and that therapy must be "potent."

118. Knittle, Beverly J., and Susan J. Tuana. "Group Therapy as Primary Treatment for Adolescent Victims of Intra-familial Sexual Abuse." *Clinical Social Work Journal* 8 (Winter 1980): 236-242.

   Describes the therapeutic needs of adolescent victims of sexual abuse, especially intrafamilial child sexual abuse. Four major needs are identified: (1) minimizing self-destructive behavior; (2) resolving emotional conflicts; (3) changing negative self-images; and (4) promoting the normal developmental tasks of adolescence. Concludes that therapy can best be presented in group therapy. The impact of incest on child victims is also discussed in some detail.

119. Koch, Michael. "Sexual Abuse in Children." *Adolescence* 15 (Fall 1980): 643-648.

   Presents a bibliographic review of English-language literature on the sexual abuse of children. Most of the items deal directly with incest, but related sex offenses are also covered. Sixteen articles are summarized. Most of the articles concern the psychological effects of incest on the child victims.

120. Krieger, Marilyn J.; Alvin A. Rosenfeld; Alan Gordon; and Michael Bennett. "Problems in the Psychotherapy

of Children with Histories of Incest." *American Journal of Psychotherapy* 34 (January 1980): 81-88.

Examines two specific issues which must be dealt with by therapists in the psychotherapy of children who have been involved in incestuous relationships. First, the therapist must be aware of the child's often "seductive presentations" in initially explaining the situation. Care must be taken to avoid being overly sympathetic or outraged. The second issue deals with more general problems, e.g., countertransference reactions, faced by therapists working with incest cases. Psychotherapists must successfully deal with these issues to establish a "therapeutic working alliance."

121. Kroth, Jerome A. "Family Therapy Impact on Intra-familial Child Sexual Abuse." *Child Abuse and Neglect* 3 (1979): 297-302.

Reports the results of an extensive statistical analysis of the family therapy treatment program used at the Child Sexual Abuse Treatment Program (CSATP) in San Jose, California. Forty-four measures of behavioral and attitudinal changes were analyzed and all that were statistically significant indicated "a positive direction with respect to the efficacy of CSATP therapy." Urges more experiments and research to determine the efficacy of various incest treatment programs. Therapists and researchers must go beyond the "psychiatric-psychoanalytic tradition of speculative, arm-chair ruminations of the intrapsychic vicissitudes of father-daughter incest."

122. LaBarbera, Joseph D., and J. Dozier. "Psychologic Responses of Incestuous Daughters: Emerging Patterns." *Southern Medical Journal* 74 (December 1981): 1478-1480.

Reviews the literature concerning the effect father-daughter incest has on the victim. Notes that many studies are contradictory and that "severe methodolic flaws further confuse the situation." Differences between short-term consequences and long-term effects are noted. Even though some research indicates that not all victims exhibit harmful side-effects, it is generally agreed that incest "amounts to significant stress for the daughter and is a form of child abuse."

123. Langsley, Donald G.; Michael N. Schwartz; and Robert H.
     Fairbairn. "Father-Son Incest." *Comprehensive
     Psychiatry* 9 (May 1968): 218-226.

     Describes a case of father-son incest and its impact
     on the individuals involved and the family as a whole.
     Differences between this homosexual type of incest and
     the more common father-daughter incest are noted. The
     individual emotional problems of the father appear to
     be more directly responsible for the development of
     this incestuous relationship with the son than the
     family interactions which typically influence hetero-
     sexual incest.

124. Layman, William A. "Pseudo Incest." *Comprehensive
     Psychiatry* 13 (July 1972): 385-389.

     Presents three case studies in which impotence or
     frigidity resulted from "pseudoincestuous relationships
     between marital partners." Because of external circum-
     stances which interrupt normal sexual relations, "the
     marital partner comes to be seen as a parent or sibling
     surrogate and, with this the universal prohibition re-
     garding incest then applies." Earlier incestuous rela-
     tions with a parent were typically found in these later
     cases of pseudo incest. Therapy techniques are briefly
     noted.

125. Lempp, Reinhart. "Psychological Damage to Children As
     a Result of Sexual Offenses." *Child Abuse and
     Neglect* 2 (1978): 243-245.

     Discusses the different types of sexual offense
     against children, including incest. Argues that in
     many cases where the acts are nonviolent, the authori-
     ties react in a way which psychologically damages the
     child victim by increasing guilt. Contends that many
     types of sexual activity between adults and children
     have not been demonstrated to be harmful. Notes, how-
     ever, that father-daughter or mother-son incest has
     harmful effects as the child matures and attempts to
     form an independent personality.

126. Lewis, Melvin, and Philip M. Sarrel. "Some Psycho-
     logical Aspects of Seduction, Incest and Rape in

Childhood." *Journal of the American Academy of Child Psychiatry* 8 (October 1967): 606-619.

Considers the relationship between actual incestuous event or rape and subsequent psychological effects on the victim. Case studies are used to describe the form of the attack and the observed impact on victims of various ages ranging from infancy to adolescence. Stresses that the type of attack greatly influences any lasting impact, but that "acute and long-term psychological sequelae may follow sexual attacks upon boys and girls during childhood." Notes that incestuous attacks occur more frequently than reported and urges therapists to explore the possibility of prior sexual attacks when dealing with adolescent patients.

127. Lukianowicz, Narcyz. "Incest." *British Journal of Psychiatry* 120 (March 1972); 301-312.

Presents two papers, one dealing with paternal incest and the second with other types of incest. Cases discussed occurred in County Antrim in Northern Ireland. The effect of father-daughter incest on the psychological development of the daughter exhibited itself in girls who became promiscuous, frigid, neurotic or who suffered no ill effects. General and personal factors of the families are considered. Personality profiles are developed for fathers, mothers, and daughters. Differences between analytical and organic theories concerning the origin of incest are briefly noted.

128. Lustig, Noel; John W. Dresser; Seth W. Spellman; and Thomas B. Murray. "Incest: A Family Group Survival Pattern." *Archives of General Psychiatry* 14 (January 1966): 31-40.

Begins with an overview of current theories on incest including contributions from anthropology, sociology and Ego psychology. Contends that incest is "one of many socially deviant behavior patterns which may be employed by a dysfunctional family in the maintenance of its own integrity and existence." Provides separate analyses of the father, mother and daughter and identifies key characteristics in the incestuous family. These characteristics include: (1) role reversal of the mother and daughter: (2) impaired sexual relations between parents; (3) maintenance of public façade; (4) fear of family disintegration; and (5) conscious or unconscious consent of the mother.

129. Macholka, Pavel; Frank S. Pittman, III; and Kalman
     Flomenhaft. "Incest as a Family Affair." *Family
     Process* 6 (March 1967): 98-116.

     Emphasizes the involvement of a non-participating
     family member, normally the mother, in cases of father-
     daughter incest. Four case studies, with lengthy
     transcripts of actual therapy sessions, are presented.
     Contends that the non-participant's denial of the in-
     cestuous activity serves to create a "family secret"
     which further complicates any resolution of the prob-
     lems created by the incest. Suggestions are made con-
     cerning appropriate therapy. Stresses the "importance
     of the mother-daughter relation in father-daughter in-
     cest."

130. Meiselman, Karin C. "Personality Characteristics of
     Incest History Psychotherapy Patients: A Research
     Note." *Archives of Sexual Behavior* 9 (June 1980):
     195-197.

     Compares sixteen female psychotherapy patients who
     had experienced incestuous relationships with sixteen
     non-incest patients who had similar backgrounds (e.g.,
     age, education, ethnic group and referring therapist).
     Results confirm the prediction that incest victims
     would report more sexual problems but do not show any
     specific link with certain expected categories of
     sexual difficulties. The Minnesota Multiphasic Person-
     ality Inventory was administered to sixteen female
     psychotherapy patients and the responses compared to
     earlier studies.

131. Miller, Virginia, and Elaine Mansfield. "Family Thera-
     py for the Multiple Incest Family." *Journal of Psy
     chiatric Nursing and Mental Health Services* 19 (April
     1981): 29-32.

     Defines incest, notes its prevalence, and briefly dis-
     cusses the incest taboo. Primarily considers three
     areas of the role of the therapist in handling incest
     cases: (1) assessment; (2) intervention; and (3) evalua-
     tion. A case study is presented to demonstrate how a
     therapist should react. Emphasizes the need for family
     therapy. Considers incest "a symptom of family malad-
     justment" and contends that therapy must be ongoing.

132. Molnar, G., and P. Cameron. "Incest Syndromes: Observations in a General Hospital Psychiatric Unit." *Canadian Psychiatric Association Journal* 20 (August 1975): 373-377.

Discusses clinical data on ten families and eight adult women involved in incestuous contacts. Notes the existence of an incest syndrome for adolescents and adults. Adolescent victims exhibit a syndrome of depressive-suicidal or runaway reactions following disclosure, while adults exhibit a syndrome of sexual disfunctions. A review of treatment methods is presented with the observation that short-term therapy was particularly effective in the treatment of adolescents. Observes that health professionals are not sufficiently aware of the incest syndrome, and that timely intervention is crucial.

133. Mrazek, David A. "The Child Psychiatric Examination of the Sexually Abused Child." *Child Abuse and Neglect* 4 (1980): 274-284.

Considers the consequences of sexual abuse and distinguishes between the child psychiatric evaluation given to a victim of incest and one conducted with a child assaulted by someone outside the family. Offers suggestions for the diagnostic process and notes the importance of assessing the immediate needs of the victim and how they can be met by social services. Difficulties in verifying the incidence and judging the likelihood of recurrence are discussed. Recommends a "supportive team approach" to deal with victims of incest and other types of sexual abuse of children.

134. Muenchow, Ann, and Edward P. Slater. "Rebuilding Families After Sexual Abuse of the Children." *Practice Digest* 1 (September 1978): 22-25.

Describes the activities of Families Reunited, a private social service agency that counsels families in which incestuous activity has occurred. Discusses how the agency coordinates its activities with the courts and local child protective services unit. Notes that the abuser must accept his guilt and the family must be willing to undergo therapy. Assertiveness training is given to both mother and child.

135. Myers, M.F. "Homosexuality, Sexual Dysfunction, and
      Incest in Male Identical Twins." *Canadian Journal
      of Psychiatry* 27 (1982): 144-147.

      Reports a unique case of incestuous activity between
      two male identical twins. Both suffered from a variety
      of sexual dysfunctions and found it difficult to live
      apart. Individual and conjoint therapy was used to
      treat both twins. Results of tests to determine physi-
      cal and psychological similarities are presented. The
      therapy is described and results are discussed. Notes
      that there is "little scientific literature on homo-
      sexual incest."

136. Nasjleti, Maria. "Suffering in Silence--The Male In-
      cest Victim." *Child Welfare* 59 (May 1980): 269-275.

      Notes that very little information is available about
      male incest victims. Since boys who are victims of in-
      cest typically remain silent, social workers in public
      agencies have little experience dealing with such vic-
      tims. Recounts group therapy experiences dealing with
      male adolescent incest victims in the Sacramento Child
      Abuse Treatment Program. Concludes that societal
      pressure is a significant reason male incest is not
      reported.

137. Panton, J.H. "MMPI Profile Configurations Associated
      with Incestuous and Non-Incestuous Child Molesting."
      Psychological Reports 45 (August 1979): 335-338.

      Assesses various personality traits of sixty-three
      male convicts, thirty-five of whom were convicted in
      incest offenses, the remaining were convicted on non-
      incestuous sexual molestation offenses involving
      children. Using the Minnesota Multiphasic Personality
      Inventory (MMPI), results indicated that incest offend-
      ers rated high on the social introversion scale. Both
      groups demonstrated the traits of despondency, in-
      security, rigidity and inhibition. Child molesters
      tended to be less mature in sexual matters.

138. Peters, J.J. "Children Who Are Victims of Sexual
      Assault and the Psychology of Offenders." *American
      Journal of Psychotherapy* 30 (July 1976): 398-421.

      Provides theoretical background, as well as seven
      case studies, of children who have been sexually

assaulted. A psychological profile of a child molester
and a description of typical victims are also provided.
Notes the extreme "psychologic confusion" which results
from incestuous sexual assaults. Emphasizes the need
for crisis intervention for child rape victims. This
is especially important because these childhood sexual
assaults can cause severe adult psychiatric problems.

139. Pittman, F.S., III. "Counseling Incestuous Families."
      Medical Aspects of Human Sexuality 10 (April 1976):
      57-58.

      Differentiates between the following types of incestu-
      ous relationships: real or imagined, overt or covert,
      unique or habitual, and structural or incidental. Suc-
      cessful therapy requires the active involvement of not
      only the victim and the offender but also the "displaced
      partner." Stresses the need for the therapist to remain
      calm and objective and to transfer this emotional re-
      sponse to the family members. Both individual and group
      family therapy are strongly recommended.

140. Poznanski, Elva, and Peter Blos, Jr. "Incest." *Medical
      Aspects of Human Sexuality* 9 (October 1975): 46-47.

      Discusses various types of overt incestuous relations
      and notes the importance of considering not only the
      two direct participants but also all other family mem-
      bers. Case studies are provided which involve father-
      daughter, mother-son, and brother-sister incest. The
      biological basis of the incest taboo and legal ramifi-
      cations are also briefly noted.

141. Quinsey, Vernon L.; Terry C. Chaplin; and Wayne F.
      Carrigan. "Sexual Preferences Among Incestuous and
      Nonincestuous Child Molesters." *Behavior Therapy* 10
      (September 1979): 562-565.

      Reports the results of an experiment in which thirty-
      six subjects, including incestuous child molesters, non-
      incestuous child molesters, and a control group, were
      shown slides of adults, pubescents and children. Penile
      circumference responses were measured. Results indicate
      that incestuous child molesters have more appropriate
      sexual age preferences than non-incestuous offenders.
      Indicates that this tends to confirm the hypothesis that
      incestuous offenders represent a special situation in
      which family dynamics play a key role.

142. Ralphling, David L.; Bob L. Carpenter; and Allen Davis.
"Incest: A Genealogical Study." *Archives of General
Psychiatry* 16 (April 1967): 505-511.

Begins with an overview of the current research on
incest covering the incidence, types, family dynamics,
and effects. Proceeds to examine a three-generation
case study involving father-daughter, mother-son and
sibling incest with special focus on the father who was
both a victim and perpetrator of incest. Observes that
the father's incestuous activity stemmed from modeling
behavior after his own father and that the mother's
behavior was passive and unconsciously consenting.
Concludes that although the cultural incest taboo is
strong, the learned values and behaviors passed down
within the family form even stronger influences.

143. Raybin, James B. "Homosexual Incest: Report of a Case
of Homosexual Incest Involving Three Generations of a
Family." *Journal of Nervous and Mental Disease* 148
(February 1969): 105-110.

Notes the absence in the literature of overt homosexual incest and examines this area by studying a
family involved in homosexual incest over three generations. A detailed case report is provided including
family background, a description of the homosexual
activity, and responses of the male family members.
It is observed that the women family members exhibited
denial. Concludes that the "family secret" of incest
served as a bond in the family and substantially dis-
torted the intrafamily roles.

144. Rhinehart, John W. "Genesis of Overt Incest." *Comprehensive Psychiatry* 2 (1961): 338-349.

Provides an extensive review of the literature on
incest and analyzes "why overt incest occurs." Four
case studies involving father-daughter, stepfather-
daughter, father-son, and brother-sister incest are
reported. In one case, the mother of a daughter involved in an incestuous relationship with the mother's
husband was the patient. A variety of general factors,
including "severe social upheaval and family disorgani-
zation," are found to contribute to overt incestuous
situations.

145. Rosenfeld, Alvin A. "A Case of Sexual Misuse." *Psychiatric Opinion* 13 (April 1976): 35-42.

Recounts a lengthy case study involving two years of therapy for an eight-year-old girl who had had an incestuous relationship with her father. Background information is provided for both parents, but the primary emphasis is on the development of a relationship between the girl and her therapist. Techniques employed in the therapy are described in some detail.

146. Rosenfeld, Alvin A. "Endogamic Incest and the Victim-Perpetrator Model." *American Journal of Diseases of Children* 133 (April 1979): 406-410.

Contends the "victim-perpetrator model," where an innocent, helpless victim is assaulted by a malevolent, physically strong perpetrator, should not automatically be used in dealing with an incestuous relationship. Family dynamics and personal interactions between everyone involved must be taken into account. Proposes a psychotherapeutic intervention technique instead of a legal and punitive reaction.

147. Rosenfeld, Alvin A. "A Historical Perspective on the Psychiatric Study of Incest." *American Journal of Forensic Psychiatry* 1 (1978): 64-79

Provides an historical overview of psychiatric theories and treatment of incest. Disagreements between Freud and Jung are considered in some detail. Major studies and works published in the decades since World War II are also discussed. Notes various factors which have forced researchers to reevaluate early estimates concerning the frequency of incestuous relationships. Recent studies have shown incest to be "a multigenerational problem in which all family members play a role." Consequently, psychotherapy is preferable to an entirely punitive approach to the problem of incest.

148. Rosenfeld, Alvin A. "Incidence of a History of Incest Among 18 Female Psychiatric Patients." *American Journal of Psychiatry* 136 (June 1979): 791-795.

Examines eighteen female psychiatric outpatients to determine the existence and incidence of incest as a factor in their case histories. Discovered that six of the patients had experienced incestuous contacts. Observed that this was a surprisingly high percentage even if half of the patients claiming incest had fan-

tasized the occurrence. Notes that there is insuffi-
cient evidence to prove that the incest itself caused
the mental illness of the patients and more research is
necessary. Recommends that therapists be more aware of
the possibility of incest in gathering the patient's
history.

149. Rosenfeld, Alvin A. "Sexual Misuse and the Family."
     Victimology: An International Journal 2 (Summer 1977):
     226-235.

     Reviews the psychiatric theories on incest, with
     special emphasis on Freud. Argues that incest is an
     extreme aspect of sexual life in the family and that
     there are healthy sexual relations between family mem-
     bers as well as unhealthy ones. Views incest as a
     form of family dysfunction and notes that when sexuality
     is well integrated into family life, a healthy family
     situation is created for the child.

150. Rosenfeld, Alvin A.; C.C. Nadelson; and M. Krieger.
     "Fantasy and Reality in Patients' Reports of Incest."
     Journal of Clinical Psychiatry 40 (April 1979): 159-
     164.

     Notes the problems encountered when a therapist must
     consider the validity of a patient's claim that incestu-
     ous relations have occurred. Eight questions are pre-
     sented which should be answered by the therapist before
     reaching any conclusions, especially when possible
     legal action is contemplated. Four important variables
     are discussed: (1) family dynamics; (2) age of the
     accuser; (3) type of sexual activity involved; and (4)
     overall quality of the reports.

151. Rosenfeld, Alvin A.; Carol C. Nadelson; Marilyn Krieger;
     and John H. Backman. "Incest and Sexual Abuse of
     Children." *Journal of the American Academy of Child
     Psychiatry* 16 (Spring 1977): 327-339.

     Uses data obtained from case studies of thirty pa-
     tients, in combination with a review of the research
     literature on incest, to assess the effects of child-
     hood incest. Among the areas covered are the following:
     (1) the legal and psychiatric problems defining incest;
     (2) literature review of incest cases and the effects
     of incestuous relationships; and (4) case reports of
     incest victims. Concludes that there are "numerous,
     complex, multidetermined variables" in considering the

effects of incest. The relationship of the participants
and the nature of the acts committed must be taken into
account.

152.   Sagatun, Inger J. "Attributional Effects of Therapy
       With Incestuous Families." *Journal of Marital and
       Family Therapy* 8 (January 1982): 99-104.

       Studies the success of Parents United, a self-help
       group which offers counseling and legal and social
       services to families in which sexual abuse has occurred.
       Fifty-six male incest offenders were given self-adminis-
       tered questionnaires. Results were examined, particular-
       ly in relation to degree of responsibility acknowledged
       by the offender, changes in family relationships, and
       recidivism. Concludes that: (1) program does increase
       sense of responsibility in both the mother and father;
       (2) actual family bonds had been disrupted by program;
       and (3) recidivism could be fully evaluated. Suggested
       further longitudinal studies.

153.   Samuels, Andrew. "Incest and Omnipotence in the Inter-
       nal Family." *Journal of Analytical Psychology* 25
       (1980): 37-57.

       Describes a case study, which reveals the relationship
       of uroboric incest and infantile omnipotence. Examines
       "phantasies attached to the loss of infantile omnipo-
       tence and then links these to uroboric incestuous phan-
       tasies implying that an individual suffering an unac-
       ceptable loss of omnipotence might experience phantasies
       of what I shall be defining as 'uroboric omnipotence'
       over and above normal omnipotent phantasies." Conse-
       quences of this condition are an inability to deal with
       people, common experience and a "numinous" life.

154.   Schneck, Jerome M. "Zooerasty and Incest Fantasy."
       *International Journal of Clinical and Experimental
       Hypnosis* 22 (October 1974): 299-302.

       Reviews a case of zooerasty involving an incest theme.
       Reports that patient had early sexual experience with
       two mares and that during hypnosis patient revealed
       that he connected the mare with his mother. Patient
       described his mother as "unapproachable" and transfered
       his feelings to the mare. Notes there is insufficient
       data to indicate the frequence of incest themes in the
       zooerastic experience.

155. Scott, Edward M. "The Sexual Offender." *International
      Journal of Offender Therapy and Comparative Criminolo-
      gy* 21 (1977): 255-263.

      Deals with case histories of sex offenders including
      victims of child molestation and incest. Notes that
      the typical offender comes from a poor or broken home,
      abuses alcohol, has strong impulses and an inadequate
      ego. Observes that prognosis for offenders who did not
      admit responsibility or guilt is far less optimistic
      than those who want to change their behavior.

156. Server, Judith Cohen, and Curtis Janzen. "Contraindica-
      tions to Reconstitution of Sexually Abusive Families."
      Child Welfare 61 (May 1982): 279-200.

      Summarizes the experience of the Sexual Abuse Treat-
      ment Programs in Baltimore City, Maryland and attempts
      to identify characteristics of the incestuous family
      which would inhibit successful reunion of family mem-
      bers following disclosure of the incest to treatment
      authorities. Accepts the premise that protection of
      the child is the first priority and argues that the
      child is at greatest risk when: (1) her report of in-
      cest is not believed by the mother; (2) the father
      denies the incest; (3) the mother is unable to protect
      the child from subsequent attacks; and (4) the parents
      are unwilling to change the family enviornment. Pro-
      vides a criteria for determining if family reconstitu-
      tion is practical.

157. Shamroy, Jerilyn A. "Perspective on Childhood Sexual
      Abuse." *Social Work* 25 (March 1980): 128-131.

      Analyzes seventy-eight cases of sexual abuse involving
      preadolescent children reported at the Children's
      Hospital Medical Center in Cincinnati, Ohio. Findings
      indicate that 72% of the abusers are known to the child.
      Recommends that abused children be approached in a non-
      judgmental manner and that a "family approach" treat-
      ment involving community agencies is the best approach
      to solving the problem. Recommends reform of the
      judicial process which tends to disturb the child.

158. Shelton, William R. "A Study of Incest." *International
      Journal of Offender Therapy and Comparative Crimi-
      nology* 19 (1975): 139-153.

      Reviews the literature on incest with special atten-
      tion to the psychology of father, mother, and daughter.

Discusses four case studies of father-daughter incest and makes observations concerning the nature of the incestuous family and the effects on family members following disclosure. Observations include: (1) legal authorities view incest as an adult sex perversion and react primarily with anger and punitive responses; (2) therapists may overreact to the incest, losing their ability to be patient and tolerant; (3) fathers perceived the incestuous act as more than physical gratification, the relationship resembling "an adolescent love affair"; and (4) because of the public uproar and shame, recidivism may not occur. Recommends the need for long-term study.

159.   Shingold, Leonard. "Some Reflections on a Case of Mother/Adolescent Son Incest." *International Journal of Psycho-Analysis* 61 (November 1980): 475-476.

Begins with a review of Freud's evolving perspective on the incest taboo and Oedipal complex. Reviews a case history of mother-son incest and discusses the nature of the incest barrier and the fear of impregnation by the son. Argues that the responsibility for incest rests primarily with the parent. Speculates that mother-son incest occurs less frequently because of "special psychic dangers" that are "phylogenetically based."

160.   Silverman, Lloyd H.; Jay S. Kwawer; Carol Wolitzky; and Mark Coron. "An Experimental Study of Aspects of the Psychoanalytic Theory of Male Homosexuality." *Journal of Abnormal Psychology* 82 (August 1973): 178-188.

Hypothesizes that "male homosexuals would show an intensification of homosexual related reactions after the subliminal presentation of an incest 'stimulus' and a decrease in such reactions after the subliminal exposure of a 'symbiosis' stimulus." Thirty-six male homosexuals were exposed to a variety of stimuli. Concludes that incest stimulus intensifies homosexual-related reactions, lending support to the theory that male homosexuality is related to incestuous wishes. Also reports that "symbiosis" stimulus has a therapeutic effect on individuals. Provides a review of literature on the relationship between psychopathology and libidinal drives.

161. Simari, C. Georgia, and David Baskin. "Incest: No
      Longer a Family Affair." *Child Psychiatry Quarterly*
      13 (April–June 1980): 36–51.

      Reviews the literature on incest. All aspects of the
      topic, from detection to treatment, are included.
      Effects on an incest victim are described using the
      example of a thirty-five-year-old woman. The involve-
      ment of all other family members is noted. Includes
      numerous references.

162. Topper, Anne B. "Options in 'Big Brother's' Involve-
      ment with Incest." *Child Abuse and Neglect* 3 (1979):
      291–296.

      Reports the results of a survey conducted of fifty-
      two teenagers and eleven adult women who had experi-
      enced incest with their fathers or stepfathers. Common
      agreement was found as to the undesirability of present
      investigation procedures which produced shame and guilt
      in the victims. Teenagers expressed disgust with their
      fathers and a desire not to know if their mothers sus-
      pected that incest was occurring. Adult women admitted
      to poor mother-daughter relations and exhibited an in-
      creasing anger toward their mothers. Adult women also
      expressed misgivings about their own abilities as
      mothers. Recommends continued judicial intervention
      but less media attention.

163. Tsai, Mauis, and Nathaniel N. Wagner. "Therapy Groups
      for Women Sexually Molested as Children." *Archives
      of Sexual Behavior* 7 (September 1978): 417–427.

      Details procedures and findings of therapy groups
      designed to treat women who had been sexually abused as
      children. An incestuous relationship was involved in
      over three-fourths of the cases. Treatments consisted
      of four sessions involving only four to six members.
      Findings included negative self-image, feelings of
      guilt and depression, mistrust of men, inadequate social
      skills, and sexual dysfunctions. Participants reacted
      positively to the support provided by the group therapy.
      Emphasizes the need to provide such therapy to adult
      women who have experienced childhood sexual assault.

164. Virkkunen, M. "Incest Offenses and Alcoholism." *Medi-
      cine, Science, and the Law* 14 (April 1974): 124–128.

      Analyzes the role alcoholism may play in incestuous
      relationships. Forty-five incest cases, of which

approximately half involved an alcoholic offender, were
studied. Alcoholics were found to have more previous
criminal records, especially those involving violent
acts. The alcoholic offender also had more frequently
been rejected by his wife as a sexual partner and this
is seen as a "contributing factor in the evolution of
the incest offence." No significant differences between
alcoholic and nonalcoholic incest offenders concerning
depression, sexual experience, psychiatric or psychotic
problems, or intelligence were found.

165. Wahl, Charles William. "Psychodynamics of Consummated
      Maternal Incest." *Archives of General Psychiatry* 3
      (July–December 1960): 188–193.

      Notes that research into incest is rare and the sub-
      ject of mother-son incest is especially unusual. De-
      scribes two cases of mother-son incest and attempts to
      identify elements within the family that would encourage
      incestuous activity. Among the elements identified are:
      (1) a rejecting mother; (2) a passive, weak father; (3)
      overt maternal seduction; (4) loss of maternal control
      through drug abuse; (5) undue physical contact between
      mother and son; (6) small age discrepancies between
      generations; and (7) presence of nonconsanguineously
      related parent. Observes that maternal incest often
      evokes in the victim disgust, disappointment, and anger
      which can cause serious damage to the ego.

166. Watts, Deborah L., and Christine A. Courtois. "Trends
      in the Treatment of Men Who Commit Violence Against
      Women." *Personnel & Guidance Journal* 60 (December
      1981): 245–249.

      Reviews treatment programs for three types of abusive
      men (rapists, incest offenders, and wife beaters), as
      reported in the published literature. Characteristics
      of the offenders are presented and certain conclusions
      drawn. Traditional psychotherapy and couples counseling
      are not as effective as behavioral programs or group
      therapy. Notes that counselors must learn to recognize
      the violence in their clients and confront the issue
      directly.

167. Weeks, Ruth B. "Counseling Parents of Sexually Abused
      Children." *Medical Aspects of Human Sexuality* 10
      (August 1976): 43–44.

      Establishes brief guidelines for therapists involved
      in counseling sexually abused children and their fami-

lies. Distinguishes between sexual attacks by
strangers or friends and incestuous activity with
relatives or members of the immediate household. Therapists must strive to prevent further trauma for the victim, especially in cases of incest. The guidelines
concern cases of sexual abuse involving a male offender.

168. Weiner, Irving B. "Father-Daughter Incest." *The Psychiatric Quarterly* 36 (1961): 607-632.

Presents five case studies of men who had had incestuous relationships with their daughters. The role of
the wives, daughters, and other children are analyzed.
Results of psychological tests given to the fathers
indicate a "striking similarity." Notes that all members of the "Oedipal triangle," father, mother, and
daughter, contribute to the overt act of incest.
Clinical literature of incest is also briefly reviewed.

169. Wells, Lloyd A. "Family Pathology and Father-Daughter
Incest: Restricted Psychopathy." *Journal of Clinical
Psychiatry* 42 (May 1981): 197-202.

Describes three types of sexual dysfunction resulting
from father-daughter incest: (1) sociopathy; (2) restricted psychopathy; and (3) family chaos. Case studies
are provided to illustrate the family behavior patterns.
Stresses the impact other members of the family, especially the mother, grandparents and other siblings, can
have on the incestuous relationship. Treatment options
are briefly considered.

170. Werman, David S. "On the Occurrence of Incest Fantasies." *Psychoanalytic Quarterly* 46 (April 1977):
245-255.

Demonstrates that incest fantasies do not necessarily
reflect severe ego or superego problems. Five brief
case studies are used to show that such fantasies can
naturally occur to nonpsychotic patients. Four factors
are identified which greatly influence these fantasies:
(1) occurrence of early and substantial sexual stimula-
tion; (2) re-emergence of these fantasies later in life;
(3) individual's tolerance of the fantasy; and (4)
awareness that some aspect of the Oedipus complex is
missing.

171. Westermeyer, Joseph. "Incest in Psychiatric Practice:
      A Description of Patients and Incestuous Relation-
      ships." *Journal of Clinical Psychiatry* 39 (August
      1978): 643-648.

      Presents a general description of the variety of
      incest patients encountered in a particular psychiatric
      practice. Few demographic differences between incest
      victims and other patients were noted. The victim typi-
      cally was significantly younger than the other partner.
      Actual intercourse was the most common sexual activity
      and some homosexual incestuous relationships were re-
      ported. Patients included both victims and offenders.

172. Yates, Alayne. "Children Eroticized by Incest." *Ameri-
      can Journal of Psychiatry* 139 (April 1982): 482-485.

      Observes that child victims of incest are traditional-
      ly perceived as passive victims of sexual assault.
      Notes that in numerous cases the child actively parti-
      cipates in the incest and exhibits highly erotic and
      seductive behavior. Asserts that the child may use the
      incest to express anger or seek nurturance and pleasure
      where no other sources are available. Presents case
      histories of eroticized children with particular atten-
      tion to the reactions of foster parents who deal with
      the child's seductive behavior. Recommends specialized
      foster parents to deal with this type of child.

173. Yorukoglu, Atalay, and John P. Kemph. "Children Not
      Severely Damaged by Incest with Parent." *Journal of
      the American Academy of Child Psychiatry* 5 (1966):
      111-124.

      Notes that in a large number of cases incest has
      severe emotional effects on the child victim. Explores
      two cases (one mother-son and one father-daughter) of
      incest where the victims remained healthy. Detailed
      case histories provided. Points out that in each case
      the child realistically viewed the parent as a seriously
      disturbed person and often played the role of parent.
      Their ability to defend themselves against serious
      trauma is attributed to the development of "healthy ego-
      functioning" before the incestuous relationships started.

174. de Young, Mary. "Siblings of Oedipus: Brothers and
      Sisters of Incest Victims." *Child Welfare* 60
      (September-October 1981): 561-568.

      Considers the reactions and problems of siblings in
      dealing with an incestuous relationship. Overall dy-

namics of an incestuous family are discussed, but the
emphasis is on the role of the other children in ac-
knowledging and handling the incest. Behavioral problems and the possibility of sibling rivalry are noted.
Two case studies are reported.

175. Zilbach, Joan J., and Margaret Galdston Grunebaum.
"Pregenital Components in Incest as Manifested in
Two Girls in Activity Group Therapy." *International
Journal of Group Psychotherapy* 14 (April 1964):
166-177.

Reviews two cases of childhood incest with special
attention to the oral stage of psychosexual development.
Activity group therapy was employed for the two patients
at the Judge Baker Guidance Center in Boston. In each
case an absence of Oedipal work was noted, with both
patients using the group activity for nurturance.
Diagnosis indicated that the problems which developed
were anchored in the oral stage and that attempts to
provide therapy on the Oedipal level would have neg-
lected an important part of the treatment.

III

SOCIOLOGICAL AND LEGAL ARTICLES

176. Adams, Morton S.; Ruth T. Davidson; and Phyllis Cornell.
"Adoptive Risks of the Children of Incest—A Pre-
liminary Report." Child Welfare 46 (March 1967):
137-142.

Examines whether children produced by incestuous relationships, either brother-sister or father-daughter,
are good adoptive risks at the age of six months.
Eighteen cases of incestuous offspring were compared
with a similar control group. The children of incest
generally had lower IQ's and other physical problems.
Only eight were recommended for adoption, as opposed to
fifteen of the control group babies. Recommends that
adoptive placements for babies from incestuous relationships be delayed to allow for adequate physical and
intelligence testing.

177. Adams, Paul L., and Gloria J. Roddy. "Language Patterns
of Opponents to a Child Protection Program." Child
Psychiatry and Human Development 11 (Spring 1981):
135-157.

Provides an analysis of various linguistic phrases
commonly used when describing incestuous acts between
father and daughter and which tend to obscure or minimize the seriousness of the act. Identifies numerous
phrases encountered while participating in a community
effort to protect children from sexual abuse. Each
phrase is placed in a lexicon and analyzed as to the
logical fallacies and rationalizations inherent in them.
Concludes that health professionals involved in the
protection of sexually abused children must be particularly aware of these phrases.

178. Anderson, Lorna M., and Gretchen Shafer. "The Charac-
      ter-Disordered Family: A Community Treatment Model
      for Family Sexual Abuse." *American Journal of Ortho-
      psychiatry* 49 (July 1979): 436-445.

      Contends that in an incestuous relationsip "the
      family unit can be seen as analogous to a 'character-
      disordered' individual." A treatment model is presented
      which is based on this consideration of the family as
      suffering from an individual "character disorder." The
      steps in the treatment are outlined and a case study
      presented. Notes that this type of treatment cannot be
      conducted on a voluntary basis but requires some sort
      of authoritative control over the offender. Urges
      further testing of the treatment model.

179. Bagley, Christopher. "Incest Behavior and Incest
      Taboo." *Social Problems* 16 (Spring 1969): 505-519.

      Examines theories of the incest taboo and identifies
      five types: (1) functional; (2) accidental; (3) patho-
      logical; (4) object fixation; and (5) psychopathic.
      Contends that the child may not be an unwilling victim
      and may initiate incest. Also contends that social
      treatment and prevention must be matched to the type
      of incest involved.

180. Bailey, Carolen F. "Incest: Practical Investigative
      Guide." *Police Chief* 46 (April 1979): 36-37.

      Observes that the reporting of incest to authorities
      is increasing and that police are generally unprepared
      to handle the situation. Reviews the steps for inter-
      viewing the child and parents and summarizes some of
      the pertinent research findings concerning incestuous
      relationships. Cautions the police investigator to be
      responsive to the child so as not to traumatize the
      child.

181. Benward, Jean, and Judianne Densen-Gerber. "Incest as
      a Causative Factor in Antisocial Behavior: An Ex-
      ploratory Study." *Contemporary Drug Problems* 4
      (Fall 1975): 323-340.

      Explores the relationship of childhood incest ex-
      perience and antisocial behavior. Interviewed 118
      women who were being treated for drug abuse at Odyssey
      House, a New York community treatment center. Dis-
      covered that 44% of those interviewed had incestuous
      experiences and 64% of the incestuous contacts were

cross-generational. Among the subsequent effects noted
were disruption of normal development, loss of self-
esteem, inability to engage in a healthy interpersonal
relationship, promiscuity, and unresolved psychic conflict. Recommends better detection, prevention, and
treatment methods with greater cooperation between
social agencies. Also urges more extensive research
on the relationship of incest to psychological and
behavioral problems.

182. Berliner, Lucy. "Child Sexual Abuse: What Happens
      Next?" *Victimology: An International Journal* 2
      (Summer 1977): 327-331.

      Points out that sexually abused children are victim-
      ized by both the abuser and social attitudes that may
      psychologically traumatize the child. Recommends
      twenty-four hour crisis counseling for immediate inter-
      vention and the involvement of child protective systems
      and the criminal justice system. A detailed outline is
      provided entitled "What If Your Child Tells You She or
      He Has Been Sexually Molested?" Explains what to do,
      common problems of abused children and effects of
      abuse and treatment.

183. Bieren, Roland E. "Incest—Still TABOO?" *Sexology* 38
      (August 1971): 55-59.

      Discusses general aspects of incest in modern society.
      Reviews the notion that the incest taboo is based on
      genetic advantages to outbreeding. Notes that there is a
      strong interest in sex within the family, but that most
      of this sexuality is repressed. Examines cases of
      homosexual, mother-son and father-daughter incest and
      reports that the incidence of sibling incest may be
      five times greater than other types.

184. Bluglass, Robert. "Incest." *British Journal of
      Hospital Medicine* 22 (August 1979): 152-156.

      Summarizes British laws against incest and analyzes
      various suggested law reforms. While agreeing that
      the current legal prohibitions need to be reformed,
      emphasizes that "there is a substantial difference be-
      tween restricting the scope of a law and abolishing it
      altogether." The prevalence of incest in Great Britain
      and a general overview of father-daughter incest are
      discussed. Suggestions for detection and treatment are
      also briefly noted.

185. Blumberg, M.L. "Child Sexual Abuse: Ultimate in Mal-
      treatment Syndrome." *New York State Journal of
      Medicine* 78 (March 1978): 612-616.

      Defines child sexual abuse and presents a description
      of typical sex offenders. Sexual involvement between
      young children and adults is often incestuous. Con-
      siders incest a "phenomenon of convenience." Class
      differences in incest are noted. Specifically, father-
      daughter incest is most common in lower-class environ-
      ments, but brother-sister incest is the most frequent
      in upper-class families. Possible causes of incest and
      the need for long-term therapy are discussed. Concludes
      that the general public needs to be better educated con-
      cerning all aspects of child sexual abuse.

186. Brooks, Barbara. "Familial Influences in Father-Daugh-
      ter Incest." *Journal of Psychiatric Treatment and
      Evaluation* 4 (1982): 117-124.

      Investigates the "family system which produces in-
      cestuous behavior." Reviews earlier research and notes
      that most studies have dealt with the individuals in-
      volved. Incest is defined and various demographic
      characteristics of incestuous families are identified.
      Clinical findings concerning fathers, mothers, and chil-
      dren in incestuous families are also presented. Concludes
      that such families are "negatively enmeshed" and are
      typically characterized by "borderline-level function-
      ing in one or more of the parties involved." Urges
      that more family studies of incest be conducted.

187. Burgess, Ann Wolbert; Lynda Lytle Holmstrom; and Maureen
      P. McCausland. "Child Sexual Assault by a Family Mem-
      ber: Decisions Following Disclosure." *Victimology:
      An International Journal* 2 (Summer 1977): 236-250.

      Reviews forty-four cases of child sexual assault by
      a family member and the decisions subsequently made on
      what to do. Discusses the circumstances of the assault,
      the motivation of the offender, how the activity is
      disclosed, decisions made by the family, and decisions
      made for the family. Notes that family loyalties are a
      source of conflict. Points out that incest must be
      viewed from the perspective of the child, the family,
      and the social agencies involved.

188. Canepa, Giacomo, and Tullio Bandini. "Incest and Family
      Dynamics: A Clinical Study." *International Journal
      of Law and Psychiatry* 3 (1980): 453-460.

      Emphasizes that researchers and therapists must con-
      sider both the overall family situation and the indi-
      viduals involved when dealing with an incestuous family.
      Presents a method of therapy using a "family dynamics"
      approach. Nine case studies of incest are discussed.
      Incest is considered a crime against the family, as well
      as the overtly affected victim. Suggests that a thera-
      peutic approach which acknowledges the interdependence
      of all family members may "disclose some of the recipe
      for incest, rather than the mere list of ingredients."

189. Carruthers, E.A. "The Net of Incest." *Yale Review* 63
      (Winter 1974): 211-227.

      Reviews the key historical works on taboos, with
      special emphasis on incest. Among the titles cited are
      Freud's *Totem and Taboo*, Ellis's *The Origins and the
      Development of the Incest Taboo*, Murdock's *Social Struc-
      ture*, and Weinberg's *Incest Behavior*. Evolutionary,
      anthropological, and behavioral approaches are general-
      ized and contrasted. Contends that, with caution, ani-
      mal studies can help us understand the nature of man.

190. Charraud, Alain; Martine Segalen; and Michel De Virville.
      "A Reply to Heider's 'Anthropological Models of Incest
      Laws in the United States.'" *American Anthropologist*
      74 (June 1972): 787-791.

      Questions both the models and data used in Heider's
      study (see #268). Statistical methods involving auto-
      matic classification are used to challenge Heider's
      contentions. Confusion in employing correct demo-
      graphic models is also noted. The data used to draw
      conclusions is itself questioned and is found to be in-
      sufficient and biased to the extent that it reflects
      only the opinions of the lawmakers who wrote the indi-
      vidual state statutes.

191. Cohen, Yehudi. "The Disappearance of the Incest Taboo."
      Human Nature 1 (July 1978): 72-78.

      Notes the current trend toward the relaxation of the
      incest taboo, particularly in Sweden. Reviews several
      theories of the origin of the taboo including the bio-
      logical theory, the natural aversion theory advanced by
      Westermarck, and the alliance theory of Lévi-Strauss.

Argues that incest taboos are greatest in the less
technological societies and quite weak where social
isolation has occurred. Asserts that in modern technological societies legal restrictions do not appear to
prevent incestuous activity and that social and emotional pressures may be the only effective way to enforce
the taboo.

192. Courtois, Christine Ann. "Incest Experience and Its
      Aftermath." *Victimology: An International Journal*
      4 (1979): 337-347.

      Summarizes interviews with thirty-one volunteer
subjects concerning their incestuous experiences in
childhood. Contends that a study of subjects who voluntarily came forward to discuss their incestuous contacts might produce different research results than
traditional studies. Among the variables studied were
duration, frequency, relatedness of participants, use
of force, undisclosed incest, disclosed incest, passive
consent of victim, and age at onset. These variables
were examined, particularly in relation to the long- and
short-term effects of the experience. Concludes that:
(1) research using traditional methodology produces
similar results; (2) age at onset and lateness of therapy involvement are correlated to severity of response;
(3) cross-generational incest may be more prevalent
than thought; and (4) each incest case must be "differ-
entially assessed, diagnosed and treated."

193. Courtois, Christine Ann. "Victims of Rape and Incest."
      Counseling Psychologist 8 (1979): 38-40.

      Identifies similarities between rape and incest but
also notes various significant differences. Duration
of involvement and family relationships are discussed.
Attacks various myths surrounding sexual victimization
of women and dealing with sexually abused girls and
women. Stresses that counselors play a critical role
in helping victims to recover. Recommended attitudes,
skills, and knowledge are identified.

194. Daugherty, Mary Katherine. "Crime of Incest Against
      the Minor Child and the States' Statutory Responses."
      Journal of Family Law 17 (November 1978): 93-115.

      Examines the various state statutes pertaining to
incest. Observes that state laws try to accomplish
two things: to regulate consanguineous marriages and to

prevent child abuse. Notes that the definitions of
incest vary widely. Some statutes may include only
parents and siblings; others may include aunts and
uncles or step-parents and children. Among the statu-
tory responses discussed are incest laws which are
supplemented by "aggravated" incest statutes which deal
with parent-child incest. Contends that most states
need to restructure their statutes and make clear what
acts are prohibited and how to deal with those acts.

195. Densen-Gerber, Judianne; Stephen F. Hutchinson; and
     Ruth M. Levine. "Incest and Drug-Related Child-Abuse:
     Systematic Neglect by Medical and Legal Professions."
     Contemporary Drug Problems 6 (Summer 1977): 135-172.

     Discusses the failure of child protective services
     to successfully protect children from abuse by parents,
     particularly parents addicted to drugs. Notes that in
     numerous cases the abuse involves incestuous contact.
     Reviews the service systems and appropriate state
     statutes in Michigan, New York, New Jersey, Massachusetts
     and Utah and provides case histories of treatment for
     each state. Recommends upgrading child protective ser-
     vices and creating criminal penalties for individuals
     who fail to report suspected child abuse. Also recom-
     mends a legal presumption of abuse or neglect when a
     parent is shown to be a drug abuser.

196. Dietz, Christine A., and John L. Craft. "Family Dy-
     namics of Incest: A New Perspective." *Social Case-
     work* 61 (December 1980): 602-609.

     Reports results of a survey conducted of protective
     service workers involved with incestuous families to
     determine if they possessed detrimental attitudes toward
     those families. Workers indicated a need for better
     training and more information on incest. In addition,
     workers felt that mothers condone incestuous relation-
     ships and that the marital relationship is poor. Recom-
     mends that schools of social work include training in
     rape, incest and spouse abuse.

197. Finkelhor, David. "Sex Among Siblings: A Survey on
     Prevalence, Variety, and Effects." *Archives of
     Sexual Behavior* 9 (June 1980): 171-194.

     Examines the prevalence and effects of sex among
     siblings based on a survey of 796 undergraduates.
     Findings include: (1) 15% of the females and 10% of

the males reported sexual experience with siblings;
(2) 25% of the sexual experiences involved force; (3)
30% felt the experience was positive and 30% negative;
(4) female participants in sibling sex are more active
sexually as young adults; and (5) sibling sex involving
force or exploitation tends to have a negative effect.
Concludes that sibling sex may not be as harmful as
first suspected. Cautions, however, that such a
finding should not be misinterpreted and that replica-
tion and further investigation are necessary.

198.   Frances, Vera, and Allen Frances. "The Incest Taboo
       and Family Structure." *Family Process* 15 (June 1976):
       235-244.

       Distinguishes between an incest barrier and an incest
       taboo. Incest barriers are established by nature and
       are represented among all animals that mate to produce
       offspring. Contends that humans have "converted an
       incest barrier inherent in our pattern of family struc-
       ture into an incest taboo." The natural basis of the
       incest barrier is combined with psychological and sym-
       bolic expressions to establish a firm incest taboo.
       Human patterns of "separation-individuation" and
       Oedipal conflict support this theory.

199.   Gentry, Charles E. "Incestuous Abuse of Children: The
       Need for an Objective View." *Child Welfare* 57 (June
       1978): 355-364.

       Examines societal attitudes toward incest. Typical
       reactions to incest by society include denial, repul-
       sion, anger, fascination with the situation. The
       response to the incestuous abuse by the victim, the
       offender and other family members is also analyzed.
       Treatment techniques are presented and the need for
       prevention emphasized. Concludes that "overall socie-
       tal attitudes and concentration on prosecution of in-
       cestuous offenders constitute barriers to prevention
       and treatment."

200.   Gibbens, T.C.N. "Sibling and Parent-Child Incest
       Offenders: A Long-term Follow-up." *British Journal
       of Criminology* 18 (January 1978): 40-52.

       Compares court cases involving father-daughter and
       brother-sister incest heard in British courts in 1951
       and 1961. Significant differences were noted between
       paternal and sibling offenders. Fathers were typically

first offenders with no criminal record and over forty.
Sibling offenders were much younger and frequently had
prior criminal convictions. Discrepancies in sentencing
were also noted. Over 90% of the fathers received
prison terms, but most sibling offenders were given non-
custodial sentences. Questions the appropriateness of
lengthy prison terms for incest offenders.

201. Goodwin, Jean M.; Doris Sahd; and Richard T. Rada.
"Incest Hoax: False Accusations, False Denials."
*Bulletin of the American Academy of Psychiatry and
the Law* 6 (1978): 269-276.

Notes the current increases in research into incest
and reports a considerable lack of data on false accusations and false denials among family members. Examines several cases covering false accusation by the
daughter, delusions of incest reported by the mother,
and false denial of daughter who retracts incest accusation usually out of guilt or fear. Concludes that
determining the truth of an incest accusation is difficult for the psychiatrist and provides guidelines for
investigation. Stresses that the investigator: (1)
must be aware of his own biases and strong feelings
toward incest; (2) should see all the family members
individually; and (3) should attempt to minimize family
trauma for the victim.

202. Greenberg, N.H. "Epidemiology of Childhood Sexual
Abuse." *Pediatric Annals* 8 (May 1979): 16.

Notes the problems inherent in trying to detect and
prevent child sexual abuse. General studies conducted
to determine the extent of such abuse are briefly summarized and the immediate and long-term effects considered. Contends that sexual abuse of children, especially that involving incest, is grossly underesti-
mated. Since no evidence can be produced to show benefits from incestuous relations, "it would be in the
best interests of the child to assume that such experiences are indeed damaging and deleterious."

203. Greene, Nancy B. "A View of Family Pathology Involving
Child-Molest--From a Juvenile Probation Perspective."
Juvenile Justice 28 (February 1977): 29-34.

Examines the current inadequacies of the California
juvenile probation departments in handling incest cases.
Focuses on the lack of information gathered on the child

and parents. Contends the child molester's wife is
frequently not asked to undergo therapy even though
she is part of the problem. Recommends that probation
departments initiate family groups and that much more
background information be gathered before decisions
are made.

204. Henderson, D.J. "Incest: Synthesis of Data." *Canadian
     Psychiatric Association Journal* 17 (August 1972): 299-
     313.

     Contends that the incest taboo is "perhaps the most
     binding moral constraint known to man." Literary
     references, epidemiological data, and anthropological
     studies are cited to justify this opinion. Theoretical
     and psychodynamic aspects of incest are also examined.
     Characteristics of typical incestuous fathers, wives
     of incestuous fathers, and daughters involved in in-
     cestuous relations are presented. Effects on partici-
     pants and factors involved in treatment are also identi-
     fied. Lengthy bibliography is included.

205. Herman, Judith Lewis. "Father-Daughter Incest." *Pro-
     fessional Psychology* 12 (February 1981): 76-80.

     Examines the issue of incest from the perspective of
     male dominance. Contends that incest is a tyrannical
     abuse of power by the father, particularly in families
     where the mother has been subjugated and the daughter
     has been socialized into traditionally submissive female
     roles. Notes that as many as one in ten women report
     sexual experiences with relatives in childhood and that
     incest often begins between the ages of six and eleven.
     Duration is often one to five years. Observes that
     wives often are victims of chronic illnesses and older
     daughters are most often at risk. Discusses various
     types of social intervention, including law enforcement,
     foster care, court-ordered rehabilitation and treatment.
     Law enforcement approaches are seen to be least helpful
     with the greatest potential for damage.

206. Herman, Judith Lewis, and Lisa Hirschman. "Families at
     Risk for Father-Daughter Incest." *American Journal of
     Psychiatry* 138 (July 1981): 967-970.

     Attempts to identify key characteristics in the family
     environment which increase the likelihood of incestuous
     contact between father and daughter. Forty female vic-
     tims of childhood incest were compared with twenty fe-

males whose fathers exhibited seductive but non-incestu-
ous behavior. Among the findings are the following:
(1) risk for incest is greatest among families where
the mother is powerless due to battering, physical or
mental disability or repeated child bearing; (2) "acting
out" behaviors of the adolescent, especially drug abuse,
suicide attempts or running away, are associated with a
high risk of incest, and (3) programs designed to counsel incestuous families should emphasize increasing the
power of the mother and strengthening her role in the
family.

207. Herman, Judith Lewis, and Lisa Hirschman. "Father-
Daughter Incest." *Signs: Journal of Women in Culture
and Society* 2 (Summer 1977): 735-756.

Examines the issue of incest from a "feminist" perspective. Notes that the incest taboo in a patriarchal
society is stronger against mother-son than father-
daughter incest. For men, incest taboo is an expression
of their property rights. Reviews clinical cases of
fifteen victims of father-daughter incest. Recommends
strengthening the mother's role in the family, providing
more protective services for women and children, and
strict enforcement of laws against sexual abuse of children. Argues that father-daughter incest will end only
after male supremacy has also ended.

208. Horowitz, Aaron Noah. "When to Intervene in Cases of
Suspected Incest." *Social Casework* 63 (June 1982):
374-375.

Questions the position put forth by Joseph Goldstein,
Anna Freud and Albert Solnit that intervention in incest
cases should occur only after criminal prosecution or
insanity has been established. Argues that health professionals should be able to conduct prior investigations where the family environment is detrimental to
the child. Admits that such investigations are intrusive
and sometimes disturb family integrity but asserts that
protecting the child's family must be balanced against
the need to protect and assist the child.

209. Hughes, Graham. "The Crime of Incest." *Journal of
Criminal Law, Criminology and Police Science* 55
(September 1964): 322-331.

Examines how the United States and England view the
crime of incest and the nature of incest itself. Among

the areas covered are: (1) a comparison of the treatment
of incest under English and U.S. law; (2) the punishment
of incest by governmental authorities; (3) the incidence
of incest and the factors which inhibit its reporting;
(4) the nature of the incest taboo; and (5) effects of
incest. Concludes that incestuous activity is harmful
and that the incest prohibition is necessary. However,
points out that present laws do not adequately deal with
the situation. Proposes a "model" incest law to improve
the legal situation. The Punishment of Incest Act of
1908 and the Sexual Offenses Act of 1956 are contrasted
with selected state laws.

210.   "Incest and Family Disorder." *British Medical Journal*
       (May 13, 1972): 364-365.

       Reviews briefly the current research on incest.
       Topics covered include: (1) the age of the perpetrator;
       (2) duration of the incestuous activity; (3) offspring
       of incestuous partners; (4) social conditions within
       the family; and (5) legal reactions to disclosures of
       incest. Recommends long-term counselling coupled with
       job training for chronically unemployed fathers.

211.   Jones, Jerry G. "Sexual Abuse of Children." *American
       Journal of Diseases of Children* 136 (February 1982):
       142-146.

       Defines and discusses three types of child abuse: (1)
       pedophilia; (2) rape and other violent assaults; and
       (3) incest. General treatment for sexually abused chil-
       dren is outlined. Notes that "incest is considerably
       more common than nonfamilial sexual abuse." Distin-
       guishes between intrafamilial, multiproblem, and acci-
       dental father-daughter incest. The psychosocial aspects
       of incest are typically more serious than the actual
       physical problems. The need for more research into
       child sexual abuse is noted.

212.   Julian, Valerie, and Cynthia Mohr. "Father-Daughter
       Incest: Profile of the Offender." *Victimology: An
       International Journal* 4 (1979): 348-360.

       Reviews a national sampling of 102 cases of father-
       daughter incest with attention directed at the charac-
       teristics of the perpetrator, the incestuous family,
       and the services provided to the families. Results
       indicate: (1) over half the victims were between the
       ages of 14-15; (2) over 90% of the households had both

parents in the family; (3) over 35% of the households
had four or more children; (4) alcoholism and mental
health problems were found to be frequently present;
(5) the majority of perpetrators are male between the
ages of 35 and 49; (6) income of incestuous families
tends to be low; (7) over 75% of incest cases received
casework counseling. Recommends that the traditional
punitive approaches toward discovery of incest is in-
correct. Such approaches often break up the family and
create guilt in the victim. Proposes social services
to improve family function.

213.   Kane, George D. "The Word That Must Be Spoken."
       American Humane Magazine 65 (December 1977): 13.

Provides a brief general update on the incidence of
incest, its effects and treatment. Notes that 41% of
reported incest cases involve victims a few weeks to /
years old and that nine out of ten victims are female.
Reports that family treatment centers are now being
established to counsel incestuous families.

214.   Kiersh, Edward. "Can Families Survive Incest?" *Cor-
       rections Magazine* 6 (April 1980): 31-38.

Discusses the development of family treatment programs as an alternative to jail terms in incest cases.
Focuses on the Child Sexual Abuse Treatment Program of
Santa Clara County (CSATP), California. Reviews the history of CSATP and the related support groups, Parents
United and Daughters United. Notes that some law enforcement personnel oppose the programs contending they
are just another form of plea bargaining and encourage
remolestation of the incest victim.

215.   Kirkwood, L.J., and M.E. Mihaila. "Incest and the Legal
       Sysetm: Inadequacies and Alternatives." *UC Davis Law
       Review* 12 (Summer 1979): 673-699.

Examines the way incest victims are treated by the
legal system. Severely criticizes the conduct of most
legal proceedings involving incest. Particular emphasis
is given to father-daughter incest. Contends that the
legal system frequently exacerbates the psychological
problems confronting the victim. Offers three specific
recommendations: (1) increased training for police offi-
cers in how to conduct interviews with sexually abused
victims; (2) assignment by the court of a lawyer to
represent the victim; and (3) establishment of more
community treatment programs.

216. Laury, G.V. "Quiz: Influences on Childhood Sexuality."
      Medical Aspects of Human Sexuality 12 (1978): 97-101.

      Provides a quiz which answers questions frequently
      raised about child sexual abuse. Certain normal aspects
      of a child's sexual development are noted and contrasted
      with unacceptable sexual activities, e.g., the natural
      desire of a young child to sleep occasionally with its
      parents is contrasted with actual incidents of overt
      incestuous activity. Notes that most girls are molested
      by someone they know and not by strangers, as commonly
      believed. Additional statistics concerning incest are
      also presented.

217. Lester, David. "Incest." Journal of Sex Research 8
      (November 1972): 268-285.

      Observes that the attitudes of researchers have often
      biased psychological research on incest. Provides a
      general review of incest research in the following areas:
      (1) frequency of occurrence; (2) incest in lower animals;
      (3) effects of incest on participants; (4) kinds of
      people who commit incest; (5) father-daughter incest;
      and (6) origin and theories of the incest taboo. Con-
      cludes that research on incest is inadequate and that
      the biases of researchers have impaired objective evalu-
      ation. Notes in particular that incestuous behavior
      may not be damaging and participants in incest may not
      be severely ill.

218. Lieske, Anna Marie. "Incest: An Overview." Perspec-
      tives in Psychiatric Care 19 (March-April 1981):
      59-63.

      Provides a general discussion of the causes, family
      dynamics, effects and treatment of incest. Observes
      that the causes of incest are complex and usually in-
      volve an emotionally dependent father who is sexually
      estranged from his wife. Points out that incest occurs
      in a dysfunctional family environment where the non-
      participants are in some way aware of the incest. In-
      cest victims have self-destructive tendencies which may
      result in truancy, suicide attempts, running away, and
      promiscuity. Discusses the factors that influence the
      severity of psychological effects on the victim and
      identifies treatment goals for the victim and family.
      Cautions health professionals about blaming the child
      for the incest because of seductive behavior on the
      victim's part.

219. Luther, Stephen L., and James H. Price. "Child Sexual
     Abuse: A Review." *Journal of School Health* 50
     (March 1980): 161-165.

     Reviews the recent literature on the sexual abuse of
     children. Discusses characteristics of the mother,
     father and child involved in incest. Attempts to define
     "child sexual abuse" and "incest" and comments on why
     this type of abuse is underreported. Provides guidance
     to health educators who encounter this problem. In-
     cludes a brief bibliography.

220. McCarty, Loretta M. "Investigation of Incest: Oppor-
     tunity to Motivate Families to Seek Help." *Child
     Welfare* 60 (December 1981): 679-689.

     Develops a model approach for investigating reported
     cases of incest. Guidelines are presented to ensure
     the safety and well-being of the victim. The appro-
     priateness of allowing the victim to remain in the home
     is also considered. Stresses the importance of the
     caseworker in initiating therapy for the entire family.
     Counseling and interview techniques are suggested.
     Notes that counselors must be able to motivate families
     to not only seek help but also continue treatment pro-
     cess.

221. McIntyre, Kevin. "Role of Mothers in Father-Daughter
     Incest: A Feminist Analysis." *Social Work* 26
     (November 1981): 462-466.

     Examines the issue of incest within the broader
     cultural context of patriarchy and male dominance.
     Criticizes researchers who identify the mother as cause
     of the incestuous activity. Argues that mothers are
     blamed because of sexist assumptions including: (1)
     mothers are supposed to be the center for nurturance;
     (2) mothers have maternal responsibility to seek ful-
     fillment at home; and (3) mothers are expected to pro-
     tect their children even if it requires them to struggle
     against their socialization to be passive and submissive.
     Contends that incest should be viewed as an abuse of
     power and dominance on the part of the father. Notes
     that patriarchy encourages incest in that the mother is
     expected to serve the father and the children are viewed
     as the father's property. Suggests a reevaluation of
     treatment alternatives based on these feminist assump-
     tions.

222. Manchester, Anthony Hugh. "The Law of Incest in England
      and Wales." *Child Abuse and Neglect* 3 (1979): 679-682.

      Examines the laws against incest in England and Wales
      and traces the legal process of a typical incest case
      from accusation by the victim, through the trial, to
      punishment and treatment of the offender and victim.
      The role of the Director of Public Prosecutions is eval-
      uated. Concludes that incest "should be retained as a
      separate criminal offence but that it should be restrict-
      ed to a narrow band of relationships."

223. Messer, Alfred A. "The 'Phaedra Complex.'" *Archives
      of General Psychiatry* 21 (August 1969): 213-218.

      Deals with the issue of stepfather-stepchild incest.
      Notes that contemporary trends indicate increases in
      broken homes and divorces, resulting in more family
      environments in which a stepfather is present. Asserts
      that it is natural for a "family romance" including some
      sexual attachment to occur as the child passes into
      adolescence. This romance is mediated by the incest
      taboo. Recommends several steps to ensure that normal
      sexual feelings do not lead to incest including: (1)
      stepfather should legally adopt the child; (2) natural
      father should be released from child support; (3) child
      should refer to parents as "mother" and "father"; and
      (4) parents should reaffirm their marital roles by
      spending time together. Contends that these steps help
      to establish a family identity and to emphasize the in-
      cest taboo.

224. Meyers, Laura. "Incest: No One Wants to Know." *Student
      Lawyer* 9 (November 1980): 28.

      Discusses a broad range of issues related to incest.
      Among the areas covered are: (1) a review of the inci-
      dence of incest; (2) an examination of the father's
      control in the incestuous family; (3) the role of the
      mother; (4) a review of treatment programs including
      CAUSES in Chicago and CSATP in California; and (5) the
      effects of incest on the child. Notes that there is
      considerable disagreement as to whether the perpetrator
      should be treated as a criminal or mentally ill. Con-
      siders the difficulties as the incest victim has in the
      legal system and cites case histories of victims and
      their decline into mental illness, delinquency and
      prostitution.

225. Nakashima, Ida I., and Gloria E. Zakus. "Incest: Review
      and Clinical Experience." *Pediatrics* 60 (November
      1977): 696-701.

      Reviews fifteen years of clinical cases at the
      Adolescent Clinic at the University of Colorado Medical
      Center. Discusses many issues including: (1) the inci-
      dence of incest; (2) definition or categories of incest;
      (3) the classic incest family; (4) sexual problems among
      the parents; (5) characteristics of the mother and child;
      (6) incestuous offspring; and (7) treatment of the in-
      cestuous family. Concludes that although family may
      appear normal, incest is a symptom of severely distorted
      family relationships.

226. Neu, Jerome. "What Is Wrong with Incest?" *Inquiry* 19
      (Spring 1976): 27-39.

      Attempts to determine what is wrong with incest.
      Cultural and biological theories of incest avoidance
      are considered but found to "neither justify nor explain
      incest taboos." Societal objections to incest are
      stated and the Oedipus complex discussed in detail.
      Concludes that while incest taboos can not be easily
      or rationally justified, "they may mark the boundaries
      that shape a way of life."

227. Nichtern S. "Effect of Sexual Disturbances on Family
      Life. *Medical Aspects of Human Sexuality* 11 (March
      1977): 116-124.

      Contends that children born out of wedlock can be
      unduly affected by the emotional and guilty reactions
      of both parents. Parental involvements with the child
      can result in various types of sexual dysfunctions and
      anxieties which may culminate in an incestuous rela-
      tionship. Father-daughter incest is much more common
      than mother-son relationships. Notes that mothers are
      generally aware of and may subconsciously condone the
      incestuous relationship between their husbands and
      daughters. Case reports involving both incest and homo-
      sexuality are presented.

228. Ordway, Dustin P. "Parent-Child Incest: Proof at Trial
      Without Testimony in Court by the Victim." *University
      of Michigan Journal of Law Reform* 15 (Fall 1981):
      131-152.

      Reviews the present judicial system's handling of incest
      cases with special attention to the inadequacies of the

present approach and its effects on the incest victim.
Argues that the child should not be asked to testify at
the trial and that this testimony be replaced by tape
recordings of pretrial examinations conducted by an
expert. Discusses the due process protections of the
defendant and concludes that the constitutional rights
of the defendant can be preserved.

229. Parker, G. "Incest." *Medical Journal of Australia* 1
      (March 30, 1974): 488-490.

Reviews Herbert Maisch's *Incest* (see #46) and generally
discusses the issue of incest. Earlier research is
briefly noted and compared to theories presented by
Maisch. Recommends the book because it correctly presents incest as both a social and family problem. Notes
that "incest is basically a fact of life."

230. Paulson, Morris J. "Incest and Sexual Molestation:
      Clinical and Legal Issues." *Journal of Clinical
      Child Psychology* 7 (Fall 1978): 177-180.

Provides a general overview of both clinical and legal
issues related to child sexual abuse. Legal rights of
children are examined and the need for legal representa-
tion and protection for incest victims is emphasized.
Examples of community-based treatment programs are described and recommended. Previous studies and published
articles are briefly summarized.

231. Price, J.M., and E.V. Valdiserri. "Childhood Sexual
      Abuse: A Recent Review of the Literature." *Journal
      of the American Medical Women's Association* 36
      (July 1981): 232-234.

Analyzes the recent literature on child sexual abuse
and draws various conclusions. Virtually all published
studies show an increase in cases but note that many
cases, especially those involving incest, are not reported. Difficulties in the detection of incestuous
child abuse are frequently noted and recommendations
identified. The studies surveyed indicate that a typical case of child sexual abuse would involve an eleven-
year-old female and her father. Possible long-term
effects are briefly considered.

232. Prince, J. "Father-Daughter Incest: An Attempt to Main-
      tain the Family and to Meet Human Needs?" *Family
      and Community Health* 4 (August 1981): 35-44.

      Considers the various psychological and societal
      factors confronting all members of an incestuous family.
      Causes of the overt incestuous activity are identified
      and the role of the mother is stressed. Notes that
      fear of family separation effectively prevents many vic-
      tims from seeking help. Therapy should combine both
      humanistic psychology and appropriate involvement of
      legal authorities. Urges the development and funding
      of programs to prevent incest.

233. Ramey, James W. "Dealing with the Last Taboo." *SIECUS
      Report* 7 (May 1979): 1.

      Raises the issue that incest may not always have
      harmful consequences. Notes that because incest is
      taboo, little research and discussion have occurred.
      Reviews some of the traditional notions and misconcep-
      tions regarding the incestuous act and argues that harm
      from incest may result more from exposure than from the
      act itself. Contends that some recent studies indicate
      that incest is not necessarily a manifestation of a
      dysfunctional family and may be healthy. Argues that
      researchers must provide the public with facts so that
      sensible and rational judgements can be made.

234. Renshaw, D.C., and R.H. Renshaw. "Incest." *Journal of
      Sex Education and Therapy* 3 (Fall-Winter 1977): 3-7.

      Outlines five major theories regarding the incest
      taboo: (1) biological; (2) psychological; (3) socio-
      logical; (4) moral; and (5) legal. Two causes for the
      breakdown of the incest taboo are also considered.
      Both personal and social factors are shown to contribute
      to the violation of the incest taboo. Concludes that
      currently no "reliable innate defenses against primary
      incest" can be readily identified. Consequently, pre-
      vention of incest is a difficult task for society.

235. Rist, Kate. "Incest: Theoretical and Clinical Views."
      American Journal of Orthopsychiatry 49 (October 1979):
      680-691.

      Reviews both theoretical and clinical approaches to
      incest. Theoretical aspects are summarized for anthro-

pological, biological, mythological and literary, and
psychoanalytic views. Clinical opinions involving family patterns, individual participants, and the impact
on participants are also considered. Various types of
treatment are briefly noted. Notes the lack of treatment reports and urges more research be conducted on all
aspects of incest.

236. Rosenfeld, Alvin A. "Sexual Abuse of Children." *JAMA:*
     Journal of the American Medical Association 240 (July
     1978): 43.

     Discusses briefly the factors leading to the sexual
     abuse of children, including incest. Proposes greater
     support for families by providing parents with more appro-
     priate ways to rear their children. The importance of
     treating not only the incestuous pair but also the non-
     participating parent is emphasized.

237. Rosenfeld, Alvin A.; Marilyn J. Krieger; Carol Nadelson;
     and John Backman. "The Sexual Misuse of Children: A
     Brief Survey." *Psychiatric Opinion* 13 (April 1976):
     6-12.

     Notes similarities and differences between physical
     abuse and sexual misuse of children. Observes that the
     former is always involved with the latter since physical
     contact is presupposed. Treatment, however, is the same
     for both, specifically family therapy. Types of child
     sexual abuse are outlined and estimates of their fre-
     quency given. Notes that parents understandably often
     try to mislead therapists about the extent of the abuse.

238. Royce, David, and Anthony A. Watts. "The Crime of In-
     cest." *Northern Kentucky Law Review* 5 (1978): 191-206.

     Examines the treatment of incest under law with par-
     ticular attention to comparing the incest statutes of
     three states: Kentucky, Ohio and New York. General
     areas discussed include: (1) the incidence of incest;
     (2) statutory analysis; (3) elements in the prosecution
     of an incest case; (4) statutory punishments of incest
     offenders; (5) duties to disclose incidents involving
     incest; and (6) causes of incest. Notes that some
     states have now broadened their laws to include step-
     parents and wards as part of the incest prohibition.
     Also observes that some protective services have been
     created to investigate incest charges. Child Protective
     Service in Cincinnati, Ohio, is discussed as a specific
     example.

239. Sagarin, Edward. "Incest: Problems of Definition and
      Frequency." *Journal of Sex Research* 13 (May 1977):
      126-135.

      Probes the different meanings of incest, particularly
      the distinction between consanguine and affinal rela-
      tionships (e.g., father-daughter versus stepfather-
      daughter incest). Proposes a distinction between "true
      incest" and "statutory incest." Discusses the types
      and variations of incest and identifies the most likely
      conditions in which a particular type of incest would
      take place. Argues that distinguishing between con-
      sanguine and affinal incest may help clarify what may
      be two distinct behaviors.

240. Sarles, Richard M. "Incest." *Pediatric Clinics of
      North America* 22 (August 1975): 633-642.

      Examines key factors in incest including: (1) the
      incidence of incest; (2) characteristics of father-
      daughter incest; (3) collusion of wives; (4) participa-
      tion of the daughter; and (5) treatment of the incestu-
      ous family. Concludes that incidence is greater than
      believed and that incest with prepubescent children
      seems to have no long-term effect, while incest with
      adolescents may be quite damaging.

241. Scheurell, Robert P., and Irwin D. Rinder. "Social
      Networks and Deviance: A Study of Lower Class Incest,
      Wife Beating, and Nonsupport Offenders." *Wisconsin
      Sociologist* 10 (Spring 1973): 56-73.

      Investigates the relationship between deviant be-
      havior and "social networks." Various theories of
      social networks are summarized and applied to three
      types of criminal offenders: incest offenders, wife
      beaters, and nonsupporters. Distinguishes between
      close-knit and loose-knit social networks and notes
      the influence the network had on various behavior pat-
      terns. Incest offenders were found to be significantly
      more socially isolated and more separated by role from
      their spouses. Concludes that "to adequately work with
      an incest offender one would manipulate the kin grouping
      by restructuring roles within the family."

242. Selby, James W.; Lawrence C. Calhoun; Joanne M. Jones;
      and Liselotte Mathews. "Families of Incest--A Collec-
      tion of Clinical Impressions." *International Journal
      of Social Psychiatry* 26 (Spring 1980: 7-16.

      Attempts to gather information on incestuous families
      by submitting a clinical inventory to a sample of social

workers. Inventory asked questions concerning the
worker's experience with incest cases. Findings include
the following: (1) incest usually is not an isolated
event, but lasts an average of one year; (2) fathers were
described as "manipulative," "impulsive," "dominating,"
and "unpredictable"; (3) daughters were described as
"passive," "emotionally dependent," and "withdrawn";
(4) mothers were seen as "meek" and "submissive"; and
(5) the family relationship was perceived as "poor."
Concludes that incest occurs in generally unhappy families where healthy roles have not been established.

243. Shepher, Joseph. "Mate Selection Among Second Genera-
      tion Kibbutz Adolescents and Adults: Incest Avoidance
      and Negative Imprinting." *Archives of Sexual Behavior*
      1 (December 1971): 293-307.

Examines premarital sexual activity and marriage patterns in an Israeli kibbutz. Avoidance was complete
and no marriages between any two members of the same
peer group were reported. The basis of this sexual
avoidance is analyzed with regard to the incest taboo.
Notes various theories and contends that incest can be
regulated in three ways: (1) inhibitions; (2) preventive
mechanisms; and (3) prohibitions. Concludes that the
problem of incest involves three variables: (1) types
of regulations; (2) types of relationships involved
(e.g., mother); and (3) evolutionary states and/or
cross-cultural types.

244. Sholevar, G. Pirooz. "A Family Therapist Looks at the
      Problem of Incest." *Bulletin of the American Academy
      of Psychiatry and the Law* 3 (March 1973): 25-31.

Observes that disclosure of incest usually leads both
the courts and the psychiatrist to deal almost exclusive-
ly with the father and that broader family dynamics are
often left unanalyzed. Examines three cases of incest
involving lower-middle-class black families. Notes
that the relationship between husband and wife was
strained with the mother uninterested in protecting
her daughter or satisfying her husband's needs. Daughters sometimes exhibited sympathy for the father and
seductive behavior. Also noted that daughter becomes
the sexual object in the family. Argues that incest
is an expression of the dysfunctional family's attempt
to manage the problems within it. Recommends that
courts and health professionals treat the family as a
whole when incest is present.

245. Simari, C. Georgia, and David Baskin. "Incest: Exploring
      the Myths." *Cornell Journal of Social Relations* 14
      (Winter 1979): 155-171.

      Presents a bibliographic overview of the major litera-
      ture on incest. Etiological issues of individual and
      familial pathological patterns are considered and the
      consequences of incest on both the victim and other
      family members are noted. Treatment and prevention
      considerations are also included. Various opinions
      concerning the origins of the incest taboo are identi-
      fied. Actual case studies are used to clarify certain
      points raised in the literature.

246. Slager, Michael "Perspective on Incest as Child-Abuse."
      Australian and New Zealand Journal of Criminology 12
      (March 1979): 3-14.

      Examines the current status of incest laws in Austra-
      lia and links incest with the broader area of sexual
      exploitation of children. Various theories related to
      the incest taboo are summarized. Causes of incest are
      categorized as psychodynamic, sociopathic, and humanis-
      tic. Implications for prevention and treatment are
      briefly noted. Concludes current laws and attitudes
      toward incest are "moth-ridden and ineffective."

247. Sklar, Ronald B. "The Criminal Law and the Incest
      Offender: A Case for Decriminalization." *Bulletin of
      the American Academy of Psychiatry and the Law* 7
      (1979): 69-77.

      Examines the perceptions and legal concepts which
      underlie incest law. Notes that the law conceives of
      the incest perpetrator as morally responsible for his
      actions and that the incestuous act is harmful to the
      victim. Observes that use of criminal law in incest
      cases creates its own harms. These include: (1) the
      possibility that criminal charges inhibit families
      from seeking counseling; (2) criminal proceedings often
      increase trauma for the family; (3) criminal law serves
      little or no therapeutic function; and (4) incest laws
      are unclear. Points out the dilemma that, while de-
      criminalization may lower conscious and unconscious in-
      hibitions to commit incest, criminal prosecution of
      incest frequently increases the family trauma.

248. Slovenko, Ralph. "Incest." *SIECUS Report* 7 (May 1979):
      4-5.

      Briefly examines how the laws in the United States
      treat incest. Notes that the trend is to broaden the

definition of incest to include a wide group of family
members, though many states still define incest in terms
of consanguine sexual relations. Remarks on the difficulties and complexities involved in employing the criminal justice system to deal with incest. Observes that
police preventive measures do not work and family members may fear retaliation if the incest is reported.
Suggests that sibling incest be decriminalized and that
other incest laws be replaced by a law of "sexual abuse
of authority." This law would include teachers and
others who regulate children.

249. Spencer, Joyce. "Father-Daughter Incest: A Clinical
     View from the Corrections Field." *Child Welfare* 57
     (November 1978): 581-590.

     Analyzes the increase in reported cases of incest and
     notes that this may "suggest a weakening of the 'taboo'
     on incest." Notes a high correlation between incest
     and certain characteristics of the father, e.g., para-
     noid personality, religious fanaticism, alcoholism, and
     doubts of masculinity. Treatment considerations and
     the additional trauma associated with hearings and
     trials are discussed. Argues that incest laws need
     to be changed "so they are based on an understanding
     of the dynamics involved."

250. Star, B. "Patterns in Family Violence." *Social Case-
     work* 61 (June 1980): 339-346.

     Reviews various aspects of family physical and sexual
     abuse, including incest. Finds many similarities in
     the different types of abusive situations. Areas
     covered include child abuse, spouse abuse, incest,
     sibling violence, spousal rape, "granny bashing," and
     parent battering. Identifies basic responsibilities
     for the social worker.

251. Strong, Bryan. "Toward a History of the Experimental
     Family: Sex and Incest in the Nineteenth-Century
     Family." *Journal of Marriage and Family* 35
     (August 1973): 457-466.

     Examines the nature of the family in the nineteenth
     century employing the two concepts of "formal family"
     and "experiential family." Areas discussed include the
     position of women, the role of sexuality, general mari-
     tal behavior, mother-child relationships (especially
     mother-son relationships), and male anxieties in the

family structure. Notes that men tended to believe
that sexual relations debased women. Particular attention is paid to incestuous attachment within the family.
Concludes that in the nineteenth century, latent incestuous attachments were encouraged and that historians
have failed to pay attention to this psychological
dimension of family life.

252.   Summit, Roland, and JoAnn Kryso. "Sexual Abuse of
        Children: A Clinical Spectrum." *American Journal of
        Orthopsychiatry* 48 (April 1978): 237-251.

        Identifies ten categories of parent-child sexuality
        and lists them in "an ascendency of apparent individual
        and social harmfulness." They are (1) incidence of
        sexual contact; (2) ideological sexual contact; (3)
        psychotic intrusion; (4) rustic environment; (5) true
        endogamous incest; (6) misogynous incest; (7) imperious
        incest; (8) pedophilic incest; (9) child rape; and (10)
        perverse incest. The effects of sexual abuse of chil-
        dren are noted. Emphasizes that "there is a vague bor-
        derline between loving sensuality and abusive sexuality."

253.   Traver, Harold Henry. "Offender Reaction, Professional
        Opinion, and Sentencing." *Criminology* 16 (November
        1978): 403-419.

        Analyzes various factors which influence the sentenc-
        ing of convicted sex offenders. Random samples of over
        350 cases of child molestation and incest arraigned
        before the Superior Courts of Los Angeles County between
        1956 and 1966 were analyzed in this study. The explana-
        tion of the offender and, specifically, if they admitted
        at least some involvement, was found to highly influence
        both the recommendation of the probation officer and the
        actual sentence imposed. Concludes that the criminal
        justice system does allow some means by which offenders
        can influence the consequences of the convictions.

254.   Tuovinen, M. "Real Incest." *Dynamische Psychiatrie* 5
        (1972): 170-178.

        Reviews earlier studies of incest and identifies
        certain external characteristics of an incest family.
        For example, in incidences of father-daughter incest
        the entire family is generally isolated from the outside
        world and the father exhibits tight control over all
        activities of the family. Stresses that in treating
        incest both parents must be considered as a unit and not
        individually. Notes that it is "the interacting combi-
        nation of parents' pathologies which is feeding the in-
        cest situation."

255. de Vos, George A. "Affective Dissonance and Primary
     Socialization: Implications for a Theory of Incest
     Avoidance." *Ethos* 3 (Summer 1975): 165-182.

     Develops a psychocultural theory of incest avoidance
     based on the concept of affective dissonance. Notes
     the universality of the incest taboo and considers both
     cultural and psychological reasons for it. Certain
     "culture-specific" problems are noted and accounted for
     by a theory of affective dissonance. Concludes that
     "some form of affective dissonance is somehow automati-
     cally at work in every society as part of intimate
     family relationships to prevent sexual arousal."

256. Weich, M.J. "The Terms of 'Mother' and 'Father' as a
     Defense Against Incest." *Journal of the American
     Psychoanalytic Association* 16 (October 1968): 783-791.

     Analyzes the linguistic development and psychological
     function of the terms "mother" and "father" as they
     relate to the incest taboo. Reviews the historical use
     of mother and father among some primitive peoples.
     Argues that the modern use of these terms serves to
     establish the parents as authorities, not just people,
     thus diverting the incest conflict. Concludes that
     "mother" and "father" play a symbolic role in "main-
     taining" and "reinforcing" the incest taboo.

257. Williams, J.E.H. "The Neglect of Incest: A Criminolo-
     gist's View." *Medicine, Science, and the Law* 14
     (January 1974): 64-67.

     Analyzes sixty-eight cases of convicted incest offend-
     ers seeking parole from British prisons in 1970-1971.
     Statistical portraits are presented for the victim and
     offender. Results of the parole hearings and prognosis
     for recovery are stated. Prison sentences of more than
     three years are felt to be unnecessary and the need for
     separate incest laws questioned. Urges further research
     on the role of the victim and emphasizes that "incest
     is a very much neglected crime."

258. DeYoung, Mary. "Innocent Seducer or Innnocently
     Seduced? The Role of the Child Incest Victim."
     Journal of Clinical Child Psychology 11 (Spring 1982):
     56-60.

     Analyzes the role of the child incest victim in
     initiating the overt incestuous relationship. Four

factors commonly cited to demonstrate "victim culpability" are presented and refuted: (1) offender's rationalizations and explanations; (2) victim passivity; (3) pre-incest sexual activity; and (4) behavior of victim during therapy. Strongly concludes that "incest is victimization; it is a reflection of adult culpability; and it is never the fault of the child."

259. Yudkin, Marcia. "Breaking the Incest Taboo: Those Who Crusade for Family 'Love' Forget the Balance of Family Power." *Progressive* 45 (May 1981): 26-28.

Examines critically the contemporary arguments advanced by some researchers that incest may have beneficial and positive effects. Notes the works of James Ramey, Joan Nelson and Seymour Parker. Contends that these individuals ignore the power dynamics that exist within the family which make consent by the child irrelevant. Argues that children have little experience in saying "no" and would have little power to terminate the relationship once begun. Regards incest, rape and child pornography as conceptually related and recommends resistance to the pro-incest researchers.

IV

ANTHROPOLOGICAL ARTICLES

260. Aberle, David, et al. "The Incest Taboo and the Mating
Patterns of Animals." *American Anthropologist* 65
(April 1963): 253-265.

Investigates the origin of the incest taboo. Various
theories concerning the origin and universality of the
incest taboo are presented and then criticized. Concludes that the human familial incest taboo is a result
of the harmful genetic effects of close inbreeding.
The taboo also solved the problem of sexual competition
within the family. Given these advantages, the incest
taboo is likely to survive as long as the family is a
viable aspect of human relations.

261. Beidelman, Thomas O. "The Filth of Incest: A Text and
Comments on Kaguru Notions of Sexuality, Alimentation
and Aggression." *Cahiers D'Etudes Africaines* 12
(1972): 164-173.

Provides the actual text and an English translation
of selected folklores concerning marriage and incest of
the Kaguru, a Bantu-speaking people of Eastern Tanzania.
The discussion of the text analyzes the basic incest
taboos expressed in Kaguru folklore. The English title
is "The Man and Wife and the People Who Could Not Defe-
cate." The plot involves sibling incest which is
gradually portrayed as a more acceptable behavior.
Urges more "ethnographic comment on similar themes by
researchers elsewhere in East Africa."

262. Burnham, Jeffrey T. "Incest Avoidance and Social
Evolution." *Mankind* 10 (December 1975): 93-98.

Examines the concept of incest avoidance in terms of
social evolution, e.g., type of social structure and
size of population. Three different "individually

operant motivational levels" are identified in societies:
(1) passive avoidance; (2) active avoidance; and (3)
taboo. Concludes that avoidance of incest originally
developed from individual sexual preferences and also
as awareness of the undesirable effects of inbreeding
became recognized by societies.

263.   Burton, Roger V. "Folk Theory and the Incest Taboo."
       Ethos 1 (Winter 1973): 504-516.

       Argues that one of the most common explanations of
       the incest taboo is sufficient itself to account for
       both its development and universality. Contends that
       the incest taboo occurred when groups of primordial
       humans recognized the harmful effects of inbreeding.
       Statistical evidence of the projected incidences of
       "bad stock" resulting from incestuous relationships is
       used to support this theory. Other social customs may
       reinforce the taboo, but it originated because man
       became aware of the "dramatically visible, deleterious
       effects of intrafamilial breeding."

264.   Coult, Allan D. "Causality and Cross-Sex Prohibitions."
       Anthropologist 65 (April 1963): 266-277.

       Presents a theory of cross-sex prohibitions, including
       both exogamy and incest. The discussion is presented
       within a framework of a "theory of causes." Material
       causes, formal causes, and efficient causes of exogamy
       within the nuclear family result from recognition of
       the "strains of in-marriage." Causes of the incest
       taboo are found to be of similar origin.

265.   Fischer, J.L.; Roger Ward; and Martha Ward. "Ponapean
       Conceptions of Incest." *Journal of the Polynesian
       Society* 85 (June 1976): 199-207.

       Examines the application of the incest taboo by the
       Micronesian people of Ponape. Notes that there are
       degrees of seriousness for incestuous relations with
       less condemnation applied to incest between more dis-
       tant clan-mates and greater condemnation applied to
       closer kin. Most serious is incest between brothers
       and sisters or parallel matrilineal first cousins. Ob-
       serves that individuals who commit incest may be ostra-
       cized and are supposed to suffer from a "supernatural
       doom" which may lead to death. Concludes that, although
       there is an incest taboo, the relative tolerance of
       Ponapeans to pre-marital and extra-marital sex leads to
       a higher incidence of incest than in many other cultures.

266. Fox, J.R. "Sibling Incest." *British Journal of Sociology* 13 (June 1962): 128-150.

Begins with an overview of the theories of incest
avoidance developed by Freud and Westermarck. Focuses
on sibling incest and reviews the nature of the incest
taboo in several cultures, including an Israeli kibbutz,
the Tallensi, the Chiricahua Apache, the Trobriand
Islanders, the Ponds, and the Tikipia. Based on this
cross-cultural analysis, the following hypothesis is
presented: "The intensity of heterosexual attraction
between cosocialized children after puberty is inversely
proportionate to the intensity of heterosexual activity
between them before puberty."

267. Frosch, William A., and Elizabeth L. Auchincloss.
"Geographic Reinforcement of the Incest Taboo: Three
Case Vignettes." *American Journal of Psychiatry* 138
(May 1981): 679-680.

Studies the relationship of geography to the presence
of an incest taboo. Notes that sexual dysfunction
occurred when adult patient was in the geographic area
of the incestuous parent. This type of "geographical
situational impotence" is discussed in terms of anthropological concepts of kinship and exogamy and the geographic supports which tend to limit incestuous relations in adulthood, e.g., newlyweds move away from
parents' home.

268. Heider, Karl G. "Anthropological Models of Incest Laws
in the United States." *American Anthropologist* 71
(August 1969): 693-701.

Compares the incest laws of the fifty states (as
amended to 1966). Notes that these state laws "seem
haphazard in their prohibitions" and are difficult to
analyze statistically. Besides the typical laws pro-
hibiting marriages with mothers, daughters, granddaugh-
ters, sisters, grandmothers, aunts, and nieces, fifteen
other incestuous relationships are prohibited in
various states. Two anthropological models are developed
to explain the differences in state incest statutes
(see also #190).

269. Hooper, Antony. "Eating Blood: Tahitian Concepts of
Incest." *Journal of the Polynesian Society* 85 (June
1976): 227-241.

Reports on a study of two small rural communities in
Tahiti which investigates Tahitian attitudes toward

incest. Examines brother-sister, second cousin and
fourth cousin incest cases. Concludes that Tahitians
view incest as a matter of degree and that the Tahitian
concepts of incest are influenced to some extent by the
current system of land tenure. In this sense, sex between kinsmen brings no new resources.

270.   Hopkins, Keith. "Brother-Sister Marriage in Roman
        Egypt." *Comparative Studies in Society and History*
        22 (July 1980): 303-354.

        Considers the incestuous marriages in Roman Egypt of
        full brothers and sisters. Contends that over one-third
        of all brothers with marriageable sisters married with-
        in the family. This direct violation of the incest
        taboo is examined in detail. A brief review of the
        anthropological, psychological, and sociological liter-
        ature on incest is presented. Historical examples of
        brother-sister marriage in Egypt are traced. Notes
        that this practice of sibling marriage directly chal-
        lenges most theories on the universality of the incest
        taboo.

271.   Huntsman, Judith, and Antony Hooper. "The 'Desecration'
        of Tokelau Kinship." *Journal of the Polynesian
        Society* 85 (June 1976): 257-273.

        Examines the concept of incest among the people of
        the Tokelau group. Indicates that Tokelaun social or-
        ganization is based on the concept of "stocks" (property
        control) and that sexual relations between kinsmen
        "confuses the categories of relationship and runs coun-
        ter to the principles upon which 'stocks' are ordered."
        Notes that Tokelaun incest prohibitions are based on
        pragmatic considerations.

272.   Kiste, Robert C., and Michael A. Rynkiewich. "Incest
        and Exogamy: A Comparative Study of Two Marshall
        Island Populations." *Journal of the Polynesian
        Society* 85 (June 1976): 209-226.

        Examines the norms and behaviors of the people of the
        Arno and Bikini atolls as they relate to incest and
        exogamy. Discusses: (1) how these two cultures differ-
        entiate kinsmen; (2) the cultural norms regulating
        marriage among permissible kinsmen; and (3) the fre-
        quency with which the norms are broken. Reviews the
        ecology, demography and history of these two populations
        and the matrilineal organization of their societies.

Concludes that breaches of norms seem far more frequent
among the people of Bikini because available sexual
partners are more limited. Observes that ecological
and demographic factors influence the systems of kinship
and marriage on these atolls.

273. Koch, Klaus-Friedrich. "Incest and Its Punishment in
      Jale Society." *Journal of the Polynesian Society* 83
      (March 1972): 84-91.

      Argues that ethnographers have "confused rules relating
      to incest, exogamy and adultery by their common failure
      to understand norms of sexual intercourse in a way that
      reflects native concepts." Takes as an example the Jale
      people of West New Guinea. Notes that the Jale consider
      incest an offense against their social order which
      may result in the execution of the perpetrator. In
      addition, the Jale believe that adverse consequences,
      such as epidemics, may strike them if incest occurs.
      Compares the Jale culture to the Yapese.

274. Kortmulder, K. "An Ethological Theory of the Incest
      Taboo and Exogamy with Special Reference to the Views
      of Claude Lévi-Strauss." *Current Anthropology* 9
      (December 1968): 437-449.

      Presents a "causal ethological theory" of the incest
      taboo. Briefly summarizes the views of Claude Lévi-
      Strauss and disagrees with certain basic tenets. How-
      ever, the theory of incest postulated is partially
      based on Lévi-Strauss' principles of gift-giving and
      redistribution. Examples of "rules of partner choice"
      found in animals are used to support this theory of
      incest.

275. Labby, David. "Incest as Cannibalism: Yapese Analysis."
      Journal of the Polynesian Society 85 (June 1976):
      171-179.

      Analyzes the incest prohibition in the Yapese culture.
      Notes that the Yaps consider incest as a form of canni-
      balism and have very strong prohibitions for incest,
      particularly regarding sexual relations with the mother.
      This is explained by noting that incest with the mother
      affects the proper reproduction of the clan and inter-
      feres with the orderly transmission of land. Notes that
      the "Yapese culture was created and perpetuated through
      the inter-relationship of the people as the sexually re-
      producing resource which maintained the land, and the
      land as the food-producing resource which maintained
      the people."

276. Makarius, Laura, and Raoul Makarius. "The Incest Prohibition and Food Taboos." *Diogenes* 30 (Summer 1960): 41-61.

Argues that the concept of kinship among primitive peoples is not fully understood in terms of lineage but may also be expanded to those who eat together. Uses this expanded view of kinship to explore the relationship of the incest taboo as it applies to those who eat together, e.g., food exogamy. Reviews the relevant factors of numerous primitive societies with particular emphasis on eating activities that separate sexes.

277. Marshall, Mac. "Incest and Endogamy on Namoluk Atoll." *Journal of the Polynesian Society* 85 (June 1976): 181-197.

Studies the concepts of incest and exogamy as applied by the Micronesian people of the Namoluk atoll. Special emphasis is placed on the ideal rules of behavior and the actual behavior of the people. Notes that the Namoluk people have different degrees of incest. Generally, incest is defined as marriage or sexual relations between individuals who treat each other as a parent, child or sibling. Genealogical distance plays an important role in the seriousness with which a particular incestuous act is treated. Author reviews the attitudes of the Namoluks toward incest violators and punishments which may result.

278. Middletown, Russell. "Brother-Sister and Father-Daughter Marriage in Ancient Egypt." *American Sociological Review* 27 (October 1962): 603-611.

Analyzes the marriage of brothers and sisters and, in some cases, fathers and daughters in ancient Egypt. Historical evidence and statistics are presented to document the prevalence of such incestuous marriages among royalty in the Pharonic and Ptolemaic periods. The most logical reason for brother-sister marriages during the period of Roman rule is the avoidance of inheritance rules. Concludes that "the evidence from ancient Egypt, particularly from the Roman period, casts doubts upon the universality of the taboo upon the marriage of brothers and sisters.

279. Monberg, Torben. "Ungrammatical 'Love' on Bellona
      (Mungiki)." *Journal of the Polynesian Society* 85
      (June 1976): 243-255.

      Studies the meaning of incest and the application of
      the taboo on the Polynesian island of Bellona. Notes
      that the taboo is strongest when it involves sexual re-
      lations with close kin. The more remote the genealogi-
      cal relation the less chance the situation will be con-
      sidered incestuous. Sanctions for incest include
      gossip, ridicule and taunt songs, but expulsion is not
      employed. Observes that although incest rules on
      Bellona are fairly clear, the rules are, in practice,
      manipulated based on the desirability of a particular
      marriage. Author provides a diagram of kinship rela-
      tions.

280. Moore, Sally Falk. "Descent and Symbolic Filiation."
      American Anthropologist 66 (December 1964): 1308-1320.

      Examines "the representation of brother and sister as
      a symbolically parental couple in descent ideology."
      List myths from various people and civilizations which
      involve incestuous creation legends. Examples are given
      where brother-sister relationships symbolically govern
      procreation of descendants, even though an actual
      marriage physically produces the children. Concludes
      that such "symbolic filiation" and descent are inter-
      woven concepts.

281. Packer, Seymour. "The Pre-Cultural Basis of the Incest
      Taboo: Toward a Biosocial Theory." *American Anthro-
      pologist* 78 (June 1976): 285-305.

      Provides an overview of the various theories relating
      to the origins of the incest taboo. Examples are dis-
      cussed which demonstrate that incest avoidance is common
      among the vertebrata and is "built into the wiring."
      Specifically, it evolved as a reaction to negative
      effects of inbreeding and as an outgrowth of increased
      intelligence and curiosity. Distinguishes between "in-
      cest taboo," a cultural prohibition and "incest avoid-
      ance," a behavioral reaction. Emphasizes the comple-
      mentary interrelationship between biology and society.

282. Proskauer, Stephen. "Oedipal Equivalents in a Clan
      Culture: Reflections on Navajo Ways." *Psychiatry*
      43 (Fall 1980): 43-50.

      Examines the Oedipal complex by contrasting the Anglo
      view of incest with the cultural traditions of the
      Navajo. Emphasis is on an examination of Navajo myth-
      ology, clan structure, and sexual relationships. Notes
      that our conventional understanding of the Oedipal
      complex is based on a nuclear family, where incest and
      rivalry are inseparable. In the Navajo culture the
      clan social structure permits an extended family where
      incest and rivalry may operate separately.

283. Rascousky, Arnaldo, and Matilde Rascousky. "The Prohi-
      bition of Incest, Filicide and the Socioculture
      Process." *International Journal of Psycho-Analysis*
      53 (May 1972): 271-276.

      Attempts to understand the process of institutional-
      izing the incest taboo through a psychoanalytic under-
      standing of filicide and parricide in primitive cultures.
      Discussion emphasizes the need of parents to control
      the aggressiveness of their children through traumatic
      restraints, including such extremes as child sacrifice
      and mutilation. Parricide is perceived as a reaction
      to this parental aggression. Through parental violence
      the incest taboo is enforced maintaining an "extreme
      paranoid condition" in the child.

284. Rehfisch, F. "Mambila Marriage Prohibitions and Incest
      Regulations and the Role System." *Journal of Asian
      and African Studies* 1 (1966): 298-309.

      Describes seven rules which regulate the choice of a
      marriage partner by prohibiting various incestuous re-
      lationships within Mambila society in Northern Nigeria.
      Examples of cases where the rules were violated are
      described and consequences to the couple noted. Argues
      that these strict marriage and incest regulations lessen
      the normal role conflicts evident in most societies.
      Concludes that these rules are "of great importance in
      the maintenance of the social structure of the Mambila
      village."

285. Ritter, Philip L. "Social-Organization, Incest, and
      Fertility in a Kosraen Village." *American Ethnologist*
      7 (November 1980): 759-773.

      Investigates a statistical decline in fertility among
      younger women from the village of Yewan on Kosrae Island

in the Eastern Carolines. This decrease could incorrect-
ly be attributed to demographic factors, such as moderni-
zation of population growth. However, an historical
study of social organization on the island reveals that
the lower fertility rates occurred because the incest
taboo was bilaterally extended to include anyone who was
considered kin during a period of depopulation. Then a
period of rapid population growth for which only a few,
atypical individuals were responsible resulted in most
current young people being related to each other and
unable to marry.

286. Rubenstein, Hymie. "Incest, Effigy Hanging, and Bi-
culturation in a West Indian Village." *American
Ethnologist* 3 (November 1976): 765-781.

Discusses the well-established ceremonial punishment
associated with the incest taboo in the coastal village
of Texier in the English-speaking, West Indian island
of St. Vincent. A mock trial followed by "hangings" of
effigies of the participants in an incestuous adult
relationship is an institutionalized ritualized method
of community justice. Notes that biculturalism is
evident because of the combination of a normal judicial
system and this lower-class custom. Two cases of incestuous relationships which resulted in "hangings"
are presented.

287. Schechner, Richard. "Incest and Culture: A Reflection
on Claude Lévi-Strauss." *Psychoanalytic Review* 58
(Winter 1971): 563-572.

Commences a discussion of the social significance of
the incest taboo by making general remarks on Claude
Lévi Strauss and his work, *The Elementary Structure of
Kinship*. Notes that Lévi-Strauss' key point was that
"sexual regulations are not independent systems but
aspects of systems of exchange." Examines the tension
that exists between the human's incestuous desires and
the biological advantage of outbreeding. Argues that
exchange is the basis of culture and that the incest
taboo serves to regulate this exchange in the face of
biological and psychological pressures to inbreed.

288. Schneider, David M. "Meaning of Incest." *Journal of
the Polynesian Society* 85 (June 1976): 149-169.

Applies an anthropological approach in defining the
concept of incest and accounting for the incest prohibition. Notes that: (1) the universality of the incest

prohibition is now open to serious doubt; (2) incest
may not be seen only as heterosexual intercourse; (3)
incest may be defined narrowly or broadly; (4) there is
a confusion between sexual intercourse and marriage,
incest and exogamy; and (5) there is a distinction between accounting for the origin of the incest taboo and
accounting for its existence in today's world. Argues
that incest is seen by societies that condemn its practice as a "desecration" that constitutes a form of
cannibalism.

289. Schwartzman, John. "The Individual, Incest, and Exoga-
      my." *Psychiatry* 37 (May 1974): 171-180.

      Discusses the development of the incest taboo by
      examining the nurturance relationship that exists be-
      tween mother and child. Argues that the mother-child
      dyad is crucial for the development of the offspring
      but that this relationship must be tempered so that the
      offspring develops an individuality and separateness.
      Argues that societies which encourage this individuality
      are more adaptive. The incest taboo encourages this
      separateness by prohibiting sexual relations among kin.
      Contends that societies with the incest taboo are,
      therefore, better able to survive.

290. Shore, Bradd. "Incest Prohibitions and the Logic of
      Power in Samoa." *Journal of the Polynesian Society*
      85 (June 1976): 275-296.

      Examines the definitions and application of the incest
      taboo and exogamy on the island of Samoa. Notes that the
      Samoan definition of incest centers on the intent of
      the individual to treat a family member as a sexual ob-
      ject. Notes that although father-daughter incest is
      strongly condemned, it is brother-sister incest which
      is central to the Samoan concept of incest. This cen-
      trality is based on the formalized relationship assigned
      brother and sisters including the brother's responsi-
      bility to protect the sister from other males. Concludes
      that "the incest prohibition reflects considerations of
      the formal power of the woman in relation to her
      brothers...."

291. Silverman, Martin G. "Relations of Production, the In-
      cest and Menstrual Tabus Among Pre-Colonial Barnabans
      and Gilbertese." *Anthropologica* 19 (1977): 89-97.

      Explores the similarities between the incest taboo
      and menstrual taboo on Barnaba Island in Micronesia.

Argues that both taboos take as an underlying principle
the relations between men and women and control over
reproduction. Incest denotes "the failure of control
over the transmission of substance from one generation
to the next. Menstruation was the failure of control
over the nontransmission of substance from one generation to the next." Applies the Marxist notion of
"simple reproduction" to this condition.

292. Smith, Alfred G., and John P. Kennedy. "The Extension
of Incest Taboos in the Woleai Micronesia." *American
Anthropologist* 62 (August 1960): 643-647.

Compares several similar societies that differ
primarily in the relatives to whom incest taboos are
applied. Inhabitants of Woleai, a group of coral islands in the west-central Carolines of Micronesia, were
studied in the 1950s. Demographic and ecological (e.g.,
distance between islands) factors were found to greatly
affect the development of incest taboos. Concludes
that incest taboos are determined by more than overall
social organization.

293. Sweetser, Dorrian Apple. "Avoidance, Social Affiliation
and the Incest Taboo." *Ethnology* 5 (July 1966):
304-316.

Attempts to characterize and explain parent-in-law
avoidance. Argues that "men avoid their parents-in-law
in societies with a strong lineal emphasis but which
have fragmented and impermanent family groups. Women
avoid their parents-in-law in the same type of situation,
and in addition they are likely to avoid if the mother's
brother has no special role to play." Notes that
parent-in-law avoidance is a symbolic recognition of
differences between consanguineal and affinal ties and
is grounded in the incest taboo and respect for parental
authority.

294. Van den Berghe, Pierre L. "Incest and Exogamy: A Sociobiological Reconsideration." *Ethology and Socio-
biology* (April 1980): 151-162.

Applies a sociobiological analysis and attempts to
update traditional anthropological explanations of the
incest taboo and exogamy. Structuralist and functional-
ist theories are reviewed with particular attention to
the theories of Lévi-Strauss. Argues that exogamy is not
an extension of incest avoidance and that there is a
fundamental distinction between the incest taboo, which

is explicitly cultural, and incest avoidance, which is
behavioral (genetic). Separates exogamy from incest
taboo or avoidance and argues that rules governing incest have no relationship with rules governing exogamy
or endogamy.

295. Van den Berghe, Pierre L., and Gene M. Mesher. "Royal
     Incest and Inclusive Fitness." *American Ethnologist*
     7 (May 1980): 300-317.

     Investigates royal incest, "the logical extreme of
     hypergyny." In stratified societies women advance by
     marrying a man of a higher class which leads to a direct
     link between high status and inbreeding. Notes that
     royal incest is a "fitness maximizing strategy," if
     three conditions are met: (1) polygyny; (2) patrilineal
     successions; and (3) parental control of royal succes-
     sion. Examples from various cultures (e.g., Ancient
     Egypt, Hawaii, and Inca Peru) are used to support
     various hypotheses derived from this theory.

296. Wagner, Roy. "Incest and Identity: A Critique and
     Theory on the Subject of Exogamy and Incest Prohibi-
     tion." *Man* 7 (December 1972): 601-613.

     Reviews the argument over whether the incest taboo
     is grounded in natural or cultural factors. Attempts
     to clarify the conflict by examining the concept of an
     incest taboo and demonstrating that the way in which a
     concept is approached and conceived is responsible, in
     part, for the conflict itself.

297. Wolf, Arthur P. "Adopt a Daughter-in-Law, Marry a
     Sister: A Chinese Solution to the Problem of the In-
     cest Taboo." *American Anthropologist* 70 (October
     1968): 864-874.

     Describes a Chinese method of circumventing the famil-
     ial incest taboo, yet maintaining continuity in existing
     domestic relationships. To avoid marriage to strangers,
     female children are adopted and raised as wives for
     their foster parents' sons. Notes that those relation-
     ships question the validity of normal sociological ex-
     planations of the incest taboo. However, this process
     is not feasible in most societies.

298. Wolf, Arthur P. "Childhood Association, Sexual Attraction, and the Incest Taboo: A Chinese Case." *American Anthropologist* 68 (August 1966): 883-896.

Analyzes the major contrasting explanations of the incest taboo as presented by psychologists and sociologists. Most psychological explanations assume early childhood sexual association depresses adult sexual attraction, while most sociological and biological theories conclude that such association increases it. A study of Chinese marriage practices in which the bride is raised from the time she is an infant by her groom's family and experiences a continual period of intimate relations from early childhood is presented. Findings support the psychosocial view and challenge the sociological explanations of the incest taboo.

299. Young, Frank W. "Incest Taboos and Social Solidarity." *American Journal of Sociology* 72 (May 1967): 589-600.

Evaluates various explanations of the incest taboo and points out their deficiencies. Redefines the incest taboo as the "prohibition of emotional alliances among persons who have been defined as ingroup members" and notes that the real basis of the taboo is "solidarity." The strength of rules of endogamy and incest prohibition directly relates to the level of familial solidarity evident in the culture. Case studies which support this "sociogenic causal explanation" are presented.

V

MEDICAL AND SCIENTIFIC ARTICLES

300. Adams, Morton S. "Incest: Genetic Considerations."
American Journal of Diseases of Children 132
(February 1978): 124.

Stresses that physicians caring for children born out
of incestuous relationships, especially brother-sister
and father-daughter incest, must be aware of this fact
to provide proper treatment. Statistically demonstrates
that such children have a higher "inbreeding intensity"
which may result in death or congenital defects. These
children may also be mentally deficient.

301. Adams, Morton S., and James V. Neel. "Children of
Incest." *Pediatrics* 40 (July 1967): 55-62.

Reports the results of a study which compared eighteen
children born as a result of incestuous relations with
a closely matched set of illegitimate children. Com-
parisons are statistically presented and analyzed. Concludes that children of incest should be considered
"high-risk" by pediatricians. Higher rates of infant
mortality and physical defects were noted for the children of incest.

302. Anderson, D., and R.W. Ten Bensel. "Counseling the
Family in Which Incest Has Occurred." *Medical Aspects
of Human Sexuality* 13 (April 1979): 143-144.

Stresses the role the family physician can play both
in early detection of incest and in its treatment. However, physicians must be receptive to the possibility
that their patients may be involved in this sort of
deviant sexual activity. It is also very important that
the physician be aware of the wide variety of social
agencies and community services which are available to
assist in the treatment of incestuous families. Guide-

lines are presented for: (1) identifying symptoms;
(2) the interview and physical examination; (3)
handling the initial crisis; and (4) reporting the
incest.

303. Bashi, Joseph. "Effects of Inbreeding on Cognitive
     Performance." *Nature* 266 (March 31, 1977): 440-442.

     Summarizes a study of over 1500 members of an Arab
     community to assess the effects of inbreeding on cogni-
     tive performance. Subjects were given both achievement
     and ability tests. Results indicated a depression for
     inbreeding in both ability and achievement. Concludes
     that there is a clear connection between genetic com-
     ponents and cognitive performance.

304. Bernstein, G.A. "Physician Management of Incest Situa-
     tions." *Medical Aspects of Human Sexuality* 13
     (November 1979): 66-87.

     Describes for physicians typical characteristics of
     incestuous families, incestuous fathers, victims, and
     mothers of female incest victims. Two case studies are
     presented to illustrate how physicians should deal with
     cases of incest. Procedures for conducting the physical
     examination of the victim are detailed and certain labo-
     ratory tests recommended. Urges physicians to become
     more aware of the problem of incest.

305. Bischof, Norbert. "The Biological Foundations of the
     Incest Taboo." *Social Science Information* 11 (Decem-
     ber 1972): 7-36.

     Explores in detail many biological and cultural
     aspects of the incest taboo. Among the areas covered
     are: (1) a cross-cultural comparison of the taboo; (2)
     a review of various theories of the taboo including a
     discussion of the biological and sociological advantages;
     (3) incest-preventing mechanisms in animals; (4) the
     biological mechanisms stimulating incest avoidance; and
     (5) incest barriers in man. Contends that instinctive
     incest barriers do exist in man, but they are "stylized
     in the framework of cultural superstructures."

306. Bixler, Ray H. "Incest Avoidance as a Function of En-
     vironment and Heredity." *Current Anthropology* 22
     (December 1981): 639-654.

     Argues that there remains an unnecessary split between
     social scientists who contend that human behavior is

environmentally determined and scientists who contend
that genetics control behavior. Uses a sociobiological
approach to review the various findings on incest avoidance. Factors considered include: (1) intimacy in
early life and its effect on mutual sexual attraction;
(2) the genetic and environmental basis of the incest
taboo; (3) close-relative inbreeding; and (4) the incidence of incest. Asserts that social scientists cannot
ignore the findings of geneticists.

307. Bixler, Ray H. "The Incest Controversy." *Psychological
      Reports* 49 (August 1981): 267-283.

      Reviews in detail the literature relating to incest
avoidance in both humans and animals. Concludes that
there are six factors which tend to inhibit incest in
human populations. These are: "(1) natural selection
which has favored outbreeding in almost all animals including our species; (2) a sexual preference continuum
which places a premium on the moderate novelty of partners; (3) the capacity of our species to recognize--or
suspect--a relationship between consanguineous mating
and defective offspring; (4) the reduction of sexual
competition and, hence, conflict in tightly knit affinal
and consanguineous family groups; (5) the nearly universal prohibition and feelings of revulsion which on
moral grounds would reduce consanguineous sexual activity and incest; and (6) the fear of punishment and dis-
approval." Notes that cultural taboos are most effective when genetic factors support the taboo.

308. Boekelheide, Priscilla Day. "Incest and the Family
      Physician." *Journal of Family Practice* 6 (January
      1978): 87-90.

      Discusses general aspects of incest with special
attention to the responsibility of the physician to
discover incestuous relations and deal effectively with
the problem. Briefly reviews the origin of the incest
taboo and the dynamics of the typical incestuous family.
Notes that the family is dysfunctional and usually includes marital problems and a mother who withdraws from
sexual and parental roles. Presents a case history of
incest and discusses clues for the family practitioner
in detecting incest. Recommends that the doctor counsel
families on a variety of matters relating to sexuality.

309. Brant, Renee S.T., and Veronica B. Tisza. "The Sexually Misused Child." *American Journal of Orthopsychiatry* 47 (January 1977): 80-90.

Reviews cases of sexual misuse reported to the emergency room of the Children's Hospital Medical Clinic in Boston over a one-year period. Considerable emphasis is placed on incestuous contacts and the need to perceive sexual abuse as a type of family pathology. Symptoms of child abuse for infants, school-age children, and adolescents are noted. Observes that there is a spectrum of child abuse ranging from sex play to violent assault. Identifies four types of high-risk children: (1) children of parents who were abused; (2) children in foster homes; (3) children who have already been abused; and (4) children of single-parent families. Recommends that in acute case management, health professionals must consider the available support system for the victim and family, the child's development in the context of the family system, the safety of the victim, and the appropriateness of the treatment.

310. Carper, John M. "Emergencies in Adolescents: Runaways and Father-Daughter Incest." *Pediatric Clinics of North America* 26 (November 1979): 883-894.

Asserts the responsibility of the pediatrician in the emergency room to deal effectively with incest victims. Discusses such issues as (1) theories underlying the reason for incest; (2) characteristics of the mother; (3) physician, nurse, or social worker attitudes toward incest; (4) diagnosis and management of the incest case; and (5) long-term effects. Argues that pediatricians must report cases and initiate treatment.

311. Cline, Foster. "Dealing with Sexual Abuse of Children." *Nurse Practitioner* 5 (May-June 1980): 52.

Briefly discusses aspects of sexual abuse of children with attention to incest victims. Makes numerous observations that would be useful to the medical practitioner. These include: (1) incidence of incest is most frequent in step-father--step-daughter relations; (2) most incest cases involve multiple sexual contacts; (3) practitioners should watch for venereal infection in small children; and (4) victims may suffer identity problems, chronic infections, or exhibit seductive behavior. Advises

careful record-keeping and cautions the practitioner
not to exhibit shock. Recommends an attitude of
receptiveness and acceptance.

312. Connell, H.M. "Incest: A Family Problem." *Medical
Journal of Australia* 2 (1978): 8362-8367.

Notes that little attention has been paid to the
sexual abuse of children. Contends that incest is part
of a pattern of "gross family pathology." Cites numerous characteristics of the incestuous family, including:
(1) large family living in overcrowded conditions; (2)
fathers poorly educated and often unemployed; and (3)
mother colluding with the father and suffering from
undue family burdens. Argues that the harmful effects
of incest are considerable and that the legal remedies
do not treat the real problem. Recommends greater
knowledge and participation by the family physician so
that incest may be prevented and effectively treated.

313. Davies, Robert. "Incest: Some Neuropsychiatric Findings." *International Journal of Psychiatry in Medicine* 9 (1978-1979): 117-121.

Analyzes the records of psychiatric inpatients at the
Yale-New Haven hospital over a ten year period. Noted
that 1.1% reported incestuous experience as children.
Other findings include: (1) seventeen of the incest
patients had abnormal EEGs; (2) five patients showed
"dull normal" IQs and seven patients gave evidence of
organicity; (3) eighteen patients had a history of
impulsivity or problems of self-awareness; (4) twelve
patients exhibited evidence of depersonalization. Contends that the neurological abnormalities present are
related to the individual's ability to form an identity
and personal boundaries. This factor, coupled with low
IQ, may increase vulnerability, especially for children.

314. Ember, Melvin. "On the Origin and Extension of the
Incest Taboo." *Behavior Science Research* 10 (1975):
249-281.

Reviews six theories about the incest taboo and concludes that only the inbreeding theory can explain the
universality of the incest prohibition. The five other
theories considered are: (1) childhood familiarity; (2)
psychoanalytic; (3) family disruption; (4) demographic;
and (5) cooperation. Detailed statistical analyses are
presented to justify the validity of the inbreeding

theory. Notes that the evidence used to support this
model suggests that "the biological problem of inbreeding may in fact explain the origin as well as the universality of the incest taboo."

315. Cowell, Elaine C. "Implications of the Incest Taboo for
Nursing Practice." *Journal of Psychiatric Nursing and
Mental Health Service* 11 (July-August 1973): 13-19.

Observes that nurses may have to deal with incest
victims and, consequently, it is important that they
have a general understanding of the psychological and
ethnographic aspects of incest. Among the areas covered
are: (1) the definition of incest; (2) the occurrence of
incest; (3) the various prohibitions on incest from
different cultures; (4) the sociological, anthropological, and psychoanalytic theories of the incest taboo;
and (5) implications for the nursing profession. Reviews the psychoanalytical and ethnographic issues and
discusses their implications for nurses. Notes that
Judaeo-Christian societies morally condemn incest and
often impose severe legal sanctions. Consequently, the
trauma which results from incest may result predominantly from the subsequent guilt rather than from the act itself. Asserts that nurses should be particularly knowl-
edgeable about the "Oedipal" periods.

316. Gross, Robert J.; Hans Doerr; Della Caldirola; Gay M.
Guzinski; and Herbert S. Ripley. "Borderline Syndrome
and Incest in Chronic Pelvic Pain Patients." *International Journal of Psychiatry in Medicine* 10 (1979-
1980): 79-96.

Conducted a multidisciplinary study of twenty-five
gynecological patients with chronic pelvic pain. Psychiatric evaluation revealed that nine of the patients
exhibited borderline syndrome, nine patients had severe
or moderate character disorders, and nine patients had
a history of childhood incest. Incest patients described conflictual relationships with either their
father or mother. Notes that there seems to be "more
than a casual association with the development of the
borderline syndrome, incest and pelvic pain."

317. Hammel, E.A.; C.K. McDaniel; and K.W. Wachter. "Demographic Consequences of Incest Tabus: A Microsimulation Analysis." *Science* (September 7, 1979): 972-977.

Employs a computer microsimulation to determine the
effects of incest taboos on the availability of "fertile

marriagable partners." Concludes that for populations
in the hundreds little effect can be found, but for
populations in the dozens the effect is considerable.

318. Herjanic, Barbara, and Ronald P. Wilbois. "Sexual Abuse
     of Children: Detection and Management." *JAMA: Journal
     of the American Medical Association* 239 (January 23,
     1978): 331-333.

     Discusses the role of the primary care physician in
     the detection and treatment of children who have been
     sexually abused. Notes that the abuser may be a family
     member and, therefore, questions must be asked concern-
     ing the home situation. Observes that the incidence of
     sexual abuse in young children is not known, but the
     physician must be suspicious when certain general symp-
     toms are found. The child must be put at ease and the
     medical interview and examination should emphasize the
     child's right to privacy and need to be relaxed. Pro-
     vides suggestions for gathering medicolegal evidence
     and measures for preventing venereal disease. Argues
     that the primary care physician may serve as the only
     advocate for the child in some circumstances, and that
     it may be the responsibility of the physician to coordi-
     nate both medical and psychosocial treatment.

319. James, Jennifer; William M. Womack; and Fred Strauss.
     "Physician Reporting of Sexual Abuse of Children."
     JAMA: Journal of the American Medical Association
     240 (September 8, 1978): 1145-1146.

     Reports responses to questionnaires mailed to a random
     sample of physicians to determine their frequency of
     contact with sexually abused children. Results indi-
     cated: (1) the most common form of abuse is father (or
     stepfather) and daughter incest; (2) there is consider-
     able trauma experienced by the child; (3) physicians
     underreport the incidences of sexual abuse; and (4)
     incest should be treated as a familial problem.

320. Kamin, Leon J. "Inbreeding Depression and I.Q." *Psy-
     chological Bulletin* 87 (May 1980): 469-478.

     Examines the validity of the concept that inbreeding
     depresses I.Q. Closely reviews the literature on the
     children of cousin marriages and incestuous matings.
     Notes that much of the research provides little or no
     evidence for the inbreeding depression of I.Q. Argues
     that authorities substantially disagree in their evalua-

tions of current data and contends that review and
popular articles often distort information on this
subject.

321. Kempe, C. Henry. "Sexual Abuse, Another Hidden Pediat-
     ric Problem: The 1977 C. Anderson Aldrich Lecture."
     Pediatrics 62 (September 1978): 382-389.

     Discusses the pediatrician's responsibility to investi-
     gate suspected incidents of incest. Points out that
     there is a reluctance to deal with this issue by doctors,
     police, and family members. Reviews the nature of sexual
     abuse, characteristics of father-daughter incest, treat-
     ment of sexual abuse, and prognosis for victims. Recom-
     mends that pediatricians openly deal with the problem.

322. Lindzey, Gerdner. "Some Remarks Concerning Incest, the
     Incest Taboo, and Psychoanalytic Theory." *American
     Psychologist* 22 (1967): 1051-1059.

     Examines the incest taboo. Distinguishes between
     "biological determinants," which are considered the
     origin of the taboo and other sociological factors,
     which are responsible for the "maintenance" of the
     taboo. Contends that the harmful biological effects of
     inbreeding favored societies that prohibited such mating
     and thus natural selection is directly responsible for
     the incest taboo. Notes that this has implications for
     successfully utilising psychotherapy in treating incest
     patients.

323. Livingstone, Frank B. "Genetics, Ecology and the Ori-
     gins of Incest and Exogamy." *Current Anthropology* 10
     (February 1969): 45-49.

     Reviews the analytical and statistical techniques for
     determining the effects of inbreeding. Attempts to
     demonstrate that biological explanations asserting
     genetic determinants for cultural universals, such as
     exogamy and the incest taboo, are inadequately sub-
     stantiated. Provides a populational and anthropological
     analysis with particular emphasis on the relation be-
     tween language acquisition and the incest taboo.

324. McCausland, Maureen P. "Sexual Development and Sexual
     Abuse: Emergencies in Adolescents." *Pediatric Clinics
     of North America* 26 (November 1979): 895-901.

     Discusses various aspects of pediatric emergencies
     involving sexual abuse, including incest. Examines such

areas as: (1) initial assessment and treatment; (2)
recording patient history; (3) obtaining consent; (4)
conducting the examination; and (5) providing therapy.
Concludes that the pediatrician is in a key position to
provide diagnosis and initiate treatment.

325. MacLean, Charles J., and Morton S. Adams. "A Method
      for the Study of Incest." *Annals of Human Genetics*
      36 (January 1973): 323-332.

      Notes that scientists have been unable to collect a
      large amount of data on close inbreeding in man. At-
      tempts to develop a method for studying close inbreeding
      by examining blood types and serum proteins of very
      young mothers and their children. Argues that these
      mothers are much more likely to have been victims of
      sibling incest and therefore provide an important group
      for study. Following a statistical analysis using
      Transitorial Matrix, concludes that undisclosed sibling
      incest provides the "minimum bias situation" for a study
      of close inbreeding. (See also #335.)

326. Moynihan, Barbara A. "Sexual Assault on the Adolescent
      Female." *Issues in Health Care of Women* 3 (January-
      February 1981): 47-54.

      Focuses on the treatment of female adolescent victims
      of sexual abuse. Guidelines and protocols are estab-
      lished for conducting the initial interview. Stresses
      that the "care of any sexual assault victim is compre-
      hensive and multidisciplinary." Identifying cases of
      incest and intervention techniques are briefly summar-
      ized. Special emphasis is placed on emergency service
      staff and nurses. Notes difficulties in dealing with
      adolescent sexual assault victims.

327. Murray, R.D. "The Evolution and Functional Significance
      of Incest Avoidance." *Journal of Human Evolution*
      (March 1980): 173-178.

      Attempts to confirm the viewpoint that cultural taboos
      against incest have a biological foundation. Reviews
      the literature on deleterious recessive genes and ex-
      plores the biological predisposition to "outbreed."
      Proposes a functional model for incest avoidance. Ar-
      gues that incest avoidance increases genetic variability
      which is essential for adaptation and is grounded in bi-
      parental reproduction. "Inbreeding in effect would
      limit the size of the effective breeding population to

levels conducive to continuous, uncontrolled genetic drift." The incest taboo is based on the advantage of this genetic variability.

328. Nakashima, Ida, and G.E. Zakus. "Incestuous Families." *Pediatric Annals* 8 (May 1979): 29-42.

Describes for medical personnel the types of symptoms frequently exhibited by incest victims and recommends various types of treatments. Incest is defined and preventive measures suggested. Characteristics of the different members of an incestuous family are identified. Concludes that "it behooves medical personnel to become aware of and alert to the possibility of its occurrence among their patients."

329. Roberts, D.F. "Incest, Inbreeding, and Mental Abilities." *British Medical Journal* (November 11, 1967): 336-337.

Remarks on current research on inbreeding and mental ability. Compiles and analyzes data on the population of Tristan da Cunha using Wright's inbreeding coefficient. Results suggest an inbreeding effect on mental ability based on "polygenic control with directional dominance."

330. Rosenfeld, Alvin A. "The Clinical Management of Incest and Sexual Abuse of Children." *JAMA: Journal of the American Medical Association* 242 (October 19, 1979): 1761-1764.

Explores various aspects in the treatment of incest victims and their families. Detection of incest is discussed in the context of four presentations: (1) genital complaints; (2) common childhood problems; (3) alterations of behavior; and (4) acting-out behaviors. Provides several recommendations for responding to an incest victim. These include speaking to the child in his own language, dealing with the problem calmly, interviewing all family members, and reporting incest cases. Emphasizes that primary care physicians must become aware of the problem and attempt to understand it fully.

331. Rubinelli, Jackie. "Incest: It's Time We Face Reality." *Journal of Psychiatric Nursing and Mental Health Services* 18 (April 1980): 17-18.

Observes that incest is a complex problem which has been compounded by the reluctance of health professionals

to deal with it. Notes that sufferers of incest are
victims of a type of rape which is further complicated
by the fact that the perpetrator is a member of the
family. Discusses both short- and long-term effects
with attention paid to dysfunctional behavior in adulthood. Recommends to health professionals that they
respond to incestuous confessions with acceptance and
empathy and be aggressive in history taking.

332. Seemanova, Eva. "A Study of Children of Incestuous
     Matings." *Human Heredity* 21 (1971): 108-128.

     Studies infant mortality and congenital defects
     occurring in 161 children resulting from incestuous
     matings. These children were compared with a control
     group comprised of children from the same mothers and
     unrelated partners. Numerous statistically significant
     differences are noted. Mortality rates for children
     from incestuous unions were much higher than those of
     the control group. Similarly, congenital deformities
     occurred more frequently among these children of incest.

333. "Sexual Survey No. 12: Current Thinking on Sexual Abuse
     of Children." *Medical Aspects of Human Sexuality* 12
     (July 1978): 44-45.

     Reports the results of a national survey of five
     hundred psychiatrists on the topic of child sexual
     abuse. Responses are statistically reported and ana-
     lyzed. Most respondents felt that: (1) victims fre-
     quently encourage the activity; (2) incest was involved
     in most cases of child sexual abuse; (3) child victims
     should be involved in a therapy program; and (4) in
     cases of father-daughter incest, the mother typically
     is aware of the activity.

334. Shapshay, Ruth, and Diane Welch Vines. "Father-Daughter
     Incest: Detection of Cases." *Journal of Psychosocial
     Nursing and Mental Health* 20 (January 1982): 23-26.

     Provides an overview of the "national problem" of
     father-daughter incest. The typical incest family is
     examined and found to be "an intact, socially isolated,
     and highly fused system." Brief case studies are used
     to describe how incest cases are disclosed and detected.
     Both physical and psychological signs of incestuous
     involvement are identified. Psychiatric nurses are
     urged to take a more active role in identifying and
     reporting cases of incest.

335.   Siskind, Victor. "Bias in Estimating the Frequency of
       Incest." *Annals of Human Genetics* 38 (January 1975):
       355-359.

       Contends that estimates of the incidence of incest in
       a given population can be inaccurate unless three vari-
       ables are considered: (1) ABO blood typing incompati-
       bility; (2) ethnic stratification; and (3) the extent
       of inbreeding in the population. Overestimating might
       result if these factors are not evaluated by the investi-
       gator. The ABO blood typing is considered the most sig-
       nificant variable, and evidence is presented to show
       that considerable overestimations could result if it is
       ignored. Responds to an earlier article by Charles
       MacLean and Morton S. Adams. (See #325.)

336.   Weeks, Ruth B. "The Sexually Exploited Child."
       Southern Medical Journal 69 (July 1976): 848-852.

       Outlines various types of child sexual abuse and
       provides a general overview of incest. Three types of
       sexual abuse are considered: (1) incest; (2) sexual
       assault; and (3) continual exploitation of children
       sexually for money or sexual perversion. Emphasis is
       on types of incest and effects on the victim. Better
       awareness by physicians, teachers and other child care
       workers to sexual abuse of children is urged.

337.   Weiner, Irving B. "A Clinical Perspective on Incest."
       American Journal of Diseases of Children 132
       (February 1978): 123-124.

       Reviews briefly the past studies on incest from the
       perspective of doctors involved in pediatric practice.
       Stresses the need for careful and individual diagnosis
       and treatment of incest victims. Normal clinical
       approaches may not be appropriate. Concludes that,
       while incest cannot be condoned, it is not necessarily
       seriously harmful to those involved.

338.   Weitzel, William D.; Barbara J. Powell; and Elizabeth C.
       Penick. "Clinical Management of Father-Daughter In-
       cest--A Critical Reexamination." *American Journal of
       Diseases of Children* 132 (February 1978): 127-130.

       Reviews the professional literature on child incest
       and presents a representative case study. Contends that
       doctors and therapists must go beyond the strictly
       physical sexual relationship in working with the victim.
       Even though separation of the offending parent and child

is frequently enforced, there is no direct evidence that an incestuous relationship is automatically harmful to the mental health of the victim. Concludes that therapeutic approaches should be employed before court action is taken, if at all possible.

339. Wilson, Jim L.; William Clements; Remi J. Cadoret; James Pease; and Ed Lammer. "The Dynamics of Incest: Presentation of One Family in Acute Crisis." *Journal of Family Practice* 7 (August 1978): 363-367.

Record of a Grand Rounds at the College of Medicine, University of Iowa. Physicians and medical students present a case of incest and discuss various aspects. Among the areas covered are: (1) family history, both psychological and physical; (2) how the incest was discovered; (3) the history of the incest taboo; (4) statistics on the frequency of incest; (5) role of the mother in father-daughter incest; (6) effects of incest on the family; and (7) treatment alternatives. Recommends a four-part treatment program which includes marriage counseling, counseling for the father, counseling for the daughter, and family counseling.

340. Woodling, Bruce A., and Peter D. Kossoris. "Sexual Misuse: Rape, Molestation, and Incest." *Pediatric Clinics of North America* 28 (May 1981): 481-499.

Defines various types of child sexual abuse and statistically describes the crime, the assailants, and the victims. A detailed procedure for the physical examination of a victim is presented. Physicians are urged to conduct a "comprehensive medicolegal evaluation." Required laboratory analyses are outlined. Differences among victims of rape, molestation, and incest are noted. Physicians must also be prepared to testify in court, but determination of sexual abuse is a "legal conclusion for the courts to decide and not a medical diagnosis."

341. de Young, Mary. "Incest Victims and Offenders: Myths and Realities." *Journal of Psychosocial Nursing and Mental Health Services* 19 (October 1981): 37-39.

Refutes various myths about incest. The following myths about incest offenders are analyzed: (1) incest only happens in "other" families; (2) the incest offender is generally psychotic; (3) the incest offender is frequently alcoholic or addicted to drugs; (4) the male

incest offender also molests children who are not
family members; and (5) sexual intercourse is usually
involved. Three misconceptions about incest victims
are also discussed: (1) victims frequently falsely
accuse family members; (2) victims often encourage the
offender by seductive behavior; and (3) the impact on
the victim is minimal. Argues that physicians and
mental health professionals "must confront the traumatic
problem of incest and assume the responsibility for
destroying the myths of incest."

VI

POPULAR ARTICLES

342. Armstrong, Louise. "The Crime Nobody Talks About."
      Woman's Day, March 1, 1978, p. 52.

      Attempts to answer some of the common questions about
      the nature of incest. Among the points raised are: (1)
      incest, unlike rape, often occurs repeatedly over a con-
      siderable span of time; (2) fathers who sexually abuse
      their children often show no other signs of abnormal
      behavior; (3) it is natural for fathers to have sexual
      feelings toward daughters; (4) severe emotional trauma
      may accompany the victim; and (5) mothers should keep
      healthy communication lines open with their daughters.

343. "Attacking the Last Taboo." *Time*, April 14, 1980, p. 72.

      Reports on the development of a pro-incest position
      among some researchers. The pro-incest position argues
      that some incestuous relationships between consenting
      family members may be beneficial or neutral, and that
      the guilt, fear, and repression are the psychological
      aspects which serve to traumatize the child. Provides
      comments from noted sex researchers such as John Money
      and Wardell Pomeroy. Notes that some researchers are
      distinguishing between "child abuse" and "consensual
      incest."

344. "Ban 'Beau Père' in Ontario—No Extenuation on French
      Film of Step-father's Incest with 14-Year-Old-Girl."
      Variety, December 2, 1981, p. 4.

      Describes the controversy surrounding the Ontario
      Censor Board's decision to ban public showings of *Beau
      Père*, a French film portraying an incestuous relation-
      ship between a stepfather and his stepdaughter. The
      opinions of the censors are quoted and reactions to the
      decision are discussed. Other films dealing with dif-
      ferent types of child sexual activity which have not
      been banned are identified.

345. Bonventre, Peter, and Marsha Zabarsky. "'I Married My
     Sister.'" *Newsweek*, July 2, 1979, p. 36.

     Reports on the case of David Goddu and Victoria Pittor-
     ino who were separated as children and adopted. Subse-
     qently, they met as adults, fell in love, and were
     married. Analyzes the application of the incest taboo
     on this couple and on the legal issues involved.

346. Brody, Jane E. "Personal Health: The Incidence of
     Incest Is Far More Common Than Most People Realize."
     New York Times, 13 June 1979, p. C8.

     Reviews the basic causes of and conditions in incestu-
     ous families. Among the points raised are: (1) three-
     fourths of the cases reported of child sexual abuse in-
     volved family members; (2) participants in incest may
     seem very normal and well-socialized individuals; (3)
     the usual victim is the eldest daughter; (4) incest may
     continue for years; (5) the father often treats the
     daughter as his "special girl"; (6) the mother may be
     abnormally dependent on the daughter; (7) victims often
     feel guilt about breaking up the family; and (8) family
     and marital counseling may help the family stay together.
     Advises that children should not share the same bed with
     parents or be exposed to casual nudity beyond the pre-
     school years.

347. "Children of Incest." *Newsweek*, October 9, 1972, p. 58.

     Discusses the research of Dr. Eva Seemanova on the
     efforts of inbreeding on the offspring. 161 children
     were examined and studied. Findings include: (1) fifteen
     of the infants were stillborn or died in the first year
     of life; (2) 40% suffered from physical or mental de-
     fects; and (3) control group infants showed significantly
     less problems. Argues that this data confirms the ad-
     verse effect of inbreeding on mortality, congenital mal-
     formations, and intelligence.

348. Cohen, Lawrence. "Swedes, Italians, Other Directors
     Break Taboo of Incest; But Few Sell." *Variety*,
     May 29, 1981, p. 38.

     Provides an historical overview of motion pictures
     which have dealt with incest. Over two hundred such
     incest films have been produced worldwide. In most
     cases the issue is peripheral to the main plot, but
     examples of movies which deal directly with incest are
     given. Notes that "very few pictures to date have dealt
     realistically with the topic." Censorship and social
     issues are also briefly discussed.

349. DeMott, Benjamin. "The Pro-Incest Lobby." *Psychology Today*, March 1980, pp. 11-18.

Examines a current trend among some academicians to discount the harmful effects of incest and to assert a positive value to some incestuous relationships. Asserts that the research supporting this view is weak and ignores basic facts about the incestuous relationship.

350. "Family Sexuality More Than 'Birds and Bees.'" *USA Today*, February 1981, pp. 7-8.

Reports on the presentations at the International Symposium on Family Sexuality held in Minnesota. Discusses James Ramey's thesis that physical affection is often withdrawn in the family once the child reaches puberty and that this withdrawl may have serious psychological consequences for the child. Argues that the fear of incest, particularly between father and daughter, leads the parents to avoid their responsibility to sexually socialize their children.

351. Greenberg, Joel. "Incest: Out of Hiding." *Science News*, April 5, 1980, pp. 218-220.

Reviews the contemporary research regarding incest including the work of David Finkelhor, Rita and Blair Justice and Benjamin DeMott. Some of the findings noted are: (1) the sexual abuse of children is more widespread than believed; (2) stepfathers are five times more likely to abuse their daughters than natural fathers; (3) the abusing father is often socially isolated; (4) the family environment is often disturbed in other ways; and (5) a high number of sexual abuse victims are abused by family members. Also reviews the theories of Freud and Lévi-Strauss as they relate to incest and summarizes the new pro-incest lobby which asserts that some incestuous contacts may be beneficial.

352. Herman, Judith Lewis. "Incest: Prevention Is the Only Cure." *Ms*, November 1981, pp. 62-64.

Discusses the need for and benefits of educating children and parents about child sexual abuse. Argues that children should receive such education early in grade school and that this education should continue and be integrated into the general sex education curricula. Cites the Hennepin County Attorney's office in Minneapolis, and the Pierce County Rape Relief program in Tacoma, Washington, as examples of good sexual abuse

education programs. Contends that, ultimately, incest
is a product of a patriarchal society, where male
dominance treats females as property.

353.   "Incest and 'Vulnerable' Children." *Science News*,
       October 13, 1979, pp. 244-245.

       Discusses the research findings of Robert Davies on
       the relationship of IQ and neurological abnormalities
       to incest occurrences. Notes that EEG abnormalities
       and "dull normal" IQ scores were found in a dispropor-
       tionately high number of subjects experiencing incest
       and that some of the abnormalities were related to the
       neurological ability to form identity. Argues that,
       although these abnormalities are unlikely to cause in-
       cest, they may make the subject more vulnerable to
       incestuous contact in the context of other family prob-
       lems.

354.   "Incest: Hidden Menace." *Family Health*, August 1978,
       p. 16.

       Reports on the research of Judith Herman and Lisa
       Hirschman of the Women's Health Collective on incest.
       Findings include: (1) most incest cases involve fathers
       and daughters; (2) incest is a product of male dominance;
       the greater the degree of male dominance, the greater
       the chance of incest; (3) victims usually were the
       eldest daughter with onset beginning between the ages
       of six and nine; and (4) victims grew into adulthood
       with poor self-images and feelings of guilt and isola-
       tion.

355.   "Incest: Personal Testimonies." *Ms*, September 1977,
       pp. 89-92.

       Consists of letters from readers of *Ms* who responded
       to a previously published article in the same magazine
       entitled "Sexual Abuse Begins at Home" (see #373).
       Letters are personal accounts of incestuous experiences,
       usually with fathers. Points out that, unlike rape,
       incest may occur repeatedly for years and that the
       victims are bound by dependency and fear. Notes that
       one girl in four has experienced sexual abuse by age 18
       and that three-fourths of the abusers are known to the
       victims.

356. "Is Incest Really Dull?" *Time*, August 24, 1970, pp. 40-41.

Article reviews the research of Arthur P. Wolf who examined incest taboos in Taiwan. Notes that early research by Edward Westermarck had demonstrated that close childhood association diminished erotic impulses. Argues that Wolf's research, which involved examining the success of marriages where the spouses were either isolated from each other or raised together in childhood, supports Westermarck's position. Remarks that Israeli kibbutz life tends also to confirm this position.

357. Janeway, Elizabeth. "Incest: A Rational Look at the Oldest Taboo." *Ms*, November 1981, p. 61.

Argues that incest is ultimately a product of a diseased family which is structured as a patriarchy. Discards the earlier theories of the incest taboo based on biological or Freudian analysis and challenges the trend developing which perceives at least some incest as a sign of healthy behavior. Contends that male dominance results in women being perceived as sex objects and submissive to male needs. This, in turn, reduces the self-image of the females and weakens family bonds. Observes that the social environment must be changed and that women must actively work toward changing family roles.

358. "Judge Sentences Brother and Sister for Marrying." *New York Times*, 2 August 1979, p. A12.

Reports on the story of David Goddu and Victoria Pittorino. Separated in very early childhood, the brother and sister married twenty years later. Judge Frances Lappin put both on probation but permitted the couple to live together so long as the relationship avoided incest.

359. Kinkead, Gwen. "The Family Secret." *Boston Magazine*, October 1977, p. 100.

Provides an extensive overview of incest in the United States with special emphasis on the treatment needs in Massachusetts. Among the areas discussed are: (1) the large incidence of incest now being reported in research and treatment centers; (2) the role played in father-daughter incest by each member of the family; (3) the

difficulties in disclosing the incestuous relationship;
(4) the available treatment programs, e.g., Child
Sexual Abuse Treatment Program, Parents United, and
Massachusetts Department of Public Welfare; and (5)
the treatment of incest by legal authorities. Recommends more foster homes, better training for health
professionals, and better treatment programs.

360. Koslow, Sally. "Incest: The Ultimate Family Secret."
      Glamour, November 1981, pp. 154-160.

      Notes that incest is "still one of the most prevalent
      forms of sexual abuse in American society—and one of
      the least understood." Comments by victims of incest
      are interspersed within this general overview of a more
      open approach to the problem and for professional
      therapy for victims.

361. Leo, John. "'Cradle-to-Grave' Intimacy." *Time*,
      September 7, 1981, p. 69.

      Discusses in a general fashion the contemporary view
      that adult-child sexual relations may be positive.
      Notes that children become sexually involved with their
      own bodies in infancy and that pre-adolescent sex play
      is a part of human and primate cultures. Includes
      counterarguments to this new view from individuals who
      argue that children cannot make a mature decision on
      whether to engage in sexual acts and the consequences
      could be psychologically and physically damaging.

362. Leo, John. "Male Dominance Revisited." *Time*, September
      22, 1980, p. 76.

      Applies the concepts of evolutionary social theory to
      the incest taboo and the dynamics of male dominance.
      Argues that there are three fundamental social groups:
      older males, females with children, and younger males
      on the periphery trying to take over from the older
      males. Contends that the struggles among these groups
      account for the incest taboo as well as hostility to
      authority, feminism, and teenage pregnancy.

363. Marks, Judi. "Incest Victims Speak Out." *Teen*.
      February 1980, p. 26.

      Presents case studies and conversations with young
      girls who have been incest victims. Incest is defined
      and general statistics presented. Notes that actual
      intercourse is attempted in only half of the cases, but

that the "psychological coercion" can have a traumatic effect on incest victims. Urges teenagers to discuss this issue and eliminate the "conspiracy of silence that protects the aggressors and conceals the victims."

364. Masters, William H., and Virginia E. Johnson. "Incest: The Ultimate Sexual Taboo." *Redbook Magazine*, April 1976, pp. 54-58.

Discusses the researchers' clinical experience with incest victims. Reviews the different types of incest, including brother-sister, father-daughter and mother-son, and notes that mother-son appears to be the most destructive and often leads to sexual dysfunction. Contends that brother-sister is least destructive and often occurs as a natural outgrowth of sexual curiosity. Observes that incest typically results in guilt, repression and shame and that its victims often experience psychological damage. Because of the stigma attached to incest, victims do not seek counselling until the trauma is severe.

365. Press, Aric; Holly Morris; and Richard Sandza. "An Epidemic of Incest." *Newsweek*, November 30, 1981, p. 68.

Observes that the incidence of incest is increasing and becoming a major public health problem. Notes that the mean age for first contact is eight years and that the incestuous relationship may go on for years. Contends that the father is often an authoritarian figure unable to function in a mature relationship with the mother, while the mother is often weak and unable to defend the child victim. Discusses the dilemma of the victim: maintaining secrecy perpetrates the activity but exposing the relationship leads to public shame and guilt and subsequently may lead to the dissolution of the family. Reviews the success of treatment programs, most notably Parents United.

366. Sawyer, Susan G. "Lifting the Veil on the Last Taboo." *Family Health*, June 1980, p. 43.

Considers incest the "most stringently forbidden sexual relationship." Quotes various authorities and studies to demonstrate that incest is "now the subject of wide-spread scientific inquiry." The phenomenal increase in incest cases is attributed to more reporting of cases, not an actual increase in the incidence of it. The effect on the victim and even the possibility of "positive incest" are briefly noted.

367. Stucker, Jan. "I Tried to Fantasize that All Fathers
Had Intercourse with Their Daughters: The Story of
Mary C." *Ms*, April 1977, p. 66.

Recounts the story of a woman who was victimized by
incest was thought to occur as a one in a million possi-
Reveals how she felt about the sexual encounters and
how she reacted to sexual exploitation. Reports that
the incest led to a serious problem with drugs and
alcohol but that most of her therapists did not know
how to treat such a patient. Argues that public attention must be paid to incest and that new techniques must
be developed in handling the complaint. Observes that,
at present, the society often views the victim as a
seductress.

368. Sulzberger, A.O., Jr. "Conferees Heard a Controversial
View of Incest." *New York Times*, 3 December 1979,
p. D9.

Reports on a controversial speech given by Professor
LeRoy G. Schultz at a conference sponsored by the
Child Sexual Abuse Victim Assistance Project. Schultz
indicated that some incest "may be either a positive,
healthy experience or at worst, neutral and dull."
Contrary opinions are noted. Reviews statistics on the
incidence of incest and discusses the possibility that
researchers assume that trauma has occurred which may
result in invalid research data. Asserts that the cause-
effect relationship between incest and trauma is weak.

369. "A Therapist Says Hush-Hush Scandal of Incest Occurs in
'Average, Respectable' Families." *People*, May 9,
1977, pp. 47-50.

Recounts an interview with Henry Giaretto, director
of the sexual abuse treatment program for the Juvenile
Probation Department of Santa Clara County. Discusses
the definition, prevalence, causes, and effects of incestuous relationships.

370. "Touch of Incest." *Time*, July 2, 1979, p. 76.

Briefly reviews the case of Victoria Pittorino and
David Goddu who were separated in childhood and subsequently fell in love and married. Discusses the attempts of the parents to seek legal action and prevent
their living as man and wife.

371. Tunley, Roul. "Incest: Facing the Ultimate Taboo."
      Reader's Digest January 1981, pp. 137–140.

      Discusses the contemporary recognition of incest as
      a serious problem. Points out that, until recently,
      incest was thought to occur as a one in a million possi-
      bility. However, recent data suggests that it might be
      as often as one in a hundred. Reviews two case studies
      and examines how some treatment programs may result in
      a return to healthy family life. Notes in particular
      the work done in Santa Clara County which has a re-
      molestation rate of less than 5%. Suggests to victims
      that they are not alone and should not hide from the act.

372. Waters, Harry F. "Does Incest Belong on TV?" *Newseek*,
      October 8, 1979, pp. 101–102.

      Discusses the controversy over a CBS dramatization of
      the book, *Flesh and Blood*, by Pete Hamill which portrays
      an incestuous relationship between mother and son. Re-
      counts protests by the National Federation for Decency
      and its attempts to influence sponsors. Asks if incest
      is an appropriate subject for television.

373. Weber, Ellen. "Sexual Abuse Begins at Home." *Ms*,
      April 1977, pp. 64–67.

      Discusses briefly many aspects of incestuous relations.
      Notes that: (1) one out of four girls are sexually
      abused by the age of 18; (2) incest occurs in families
      of all social and economic backgrounds; (3) the average
      age of sexual abuse is 11 years old; (4) women who have
      been sexually abused have problems in adult life; and
      (5) 34% of sexual molestations occur in the home. Ex-
      amines the treatment programs available, with special
      attention to the Santa Clara Child Sexual Abuse Treat-
      ment Program. Observes that the taboo toward family
      sex serves to increase its secrecy and consequently
      inability of society to deal with the problem. (See
      also #355.)

VII

LITERARY ARTICLES

374. Aggeler, Geoffrey. "Incest and the Artist: Anthony
     Burgess's MF as Summation." *Modern Fiction Studies*
     18 (Winter 1972-73): 529-543.

     Describes how Anthony Burgess uses both Indian and
     Greek incest myths in his novel *MF*, published in 1971.
     The influence on Burgess of Lévi-Strauss and his theo-
     ries relating to incest and riddles is closely examined.
     Specfic references to Algonquian Indian and Oedipal in-
     cest myths are presented. The plot of the novel is
     briefly summarized. Concludes that "Riddling and incest
     have become associated in myth because they are both
     frustration of natural expectations."

375. Barnett, Louise R. "American Novelists and the "Por-
     trait of Beatrice Cenci." *New England Quarterly* 53
     (June 1980): 168-183.

     Compares the use of a famous painting, Beatrice Cenci,
     as a symbol of incest in the works of three major
     American novelists. The background of the portrait is
     explained and its treatment in Melville's *Pierce*, Haw-
     thorne's *The Marble Faun*, and Wharton's *The House of
     Mirth* examined. Differences are noted, but concludes
     that "all found it a means of evoking the theme of in-
     cest, which contemporary canons of decorum kept from
     open discussion."

376. Battestin, Martin C. "Henry Fielding, Sarah Fielding,
     and 'the dreadful Sin of Incest.'" *Novel: A Forum
     on Fiction* 13 (Fall 1979): 6-18.

     Notes that, although Fielding wrote comedies, the
     serious theme of the "sin of incest" appears in several
     of his works, most notably, *Joseph Andrews* and *Tom Jones*.
     Asserts that novels and other artistic works are not

only products of creativity but of the conscious and
unconscious motivations of the author. Proposes that
an explanation of the incest theme, therefore, requires
a biographical as well as literary explanation. Discusses Fielding's childhood, particularly his relationship with his sister Sarah. Provides a psychological
analysis which recognizes Fielding's lack of a mother
and father, the excesses of a doting aunt, and sexual
experimentation with this sister.

377. Brophy, Robert J. "'Tamar,' 'The Cenci,' and Incest."
      *American Literature: A Journal of Literary History,
      Criticism, and Bibliography* 42 (May 1970): 241-244.

      Cites parallels between Robinson Jeffers' verse narra-
      tive "Tamar" and Shelley's *The Cenci*. Thematic compari-
      sons are made and virtually identical dramatic struc-
      tures and allusions noted. Contends that incest "serves
      as a metaphor in both dramas, partly for what civiliza-
      tion has wrought in terms of self-regarding, inverted
      values and institutions, partly for the mold-breaking,
      transcendent repercussions precipitated by the act."
      Concludes that the mark of a "true poet" is the ability
      to "make even the most degraded and negative into a
      positive revelatory device."

378. Dervin, Daniel A. "The Spook in the Rainforest: The
      Incestuous Structure of Tennessee Williams's Plays."
      *Psychocultural Review: Interpretations in the Psy-
      chology of Art, Literature and Society* 3 (Summer-Fall
      1979): 153-183.

      Examines the themes of several Tennessee Williams
      plays with special emphasis on incestuous themes which
      relate both to the playwright and the plays themselves.
      Employs an analytical tool in which the plays are seen
      as being produced by "a central recurring character,"
      who produces the plays from three psychic states--
      memory, fantasy and dream. Notes that incest is direct-
      ly dealt with in *The Glass Menagerie* and *The Purifica-
      tion*, and indirectly discovered in plays such as *The
      Rose Tattoo*, *You Touched Me* and *Orpheus Descending*.

379. Durbach, Errol. "The Geschwister-Komplex: Romantic
      Attitudes to Brother-Sister Incest in Ibsen, Byron
      and Emily Bronte." *Mosaic: A Journal for the Compara-
      tive Study of Literature and Ideas* 12 (Summer 1979):
      61-73.

      Focuses on Ibsen and compares the treatment of incest
      in Ibsen's *Little Eyolf*, Byron's *Cain* and Emily Brontë's

Wuthering Heights. Asserts that Ibsen's contribution
was to make the Romantic concept of incest "fully ar-
ticulate, and in this way to expose consciously the
human offensiveness of an erotic ideal which ultimately
insulates the idealist against love in all its forms...."
Employs the works of Byron and Brontë as exemplars of
the Romantic and post-Romantic period in their treatment
of the incest theme.

380. Erlich, Gloria C. "Hawthorne and the Mannings."
Studies in the American Renaissance (1980): 97-117.

Investigates, in great biographical detail, the effects his maternal ancestors, namely the Manning family,
may have had on Nathaniel Hawthorne. Particular emphasis is given to an incident of brother-sister incest
which occurred in 1680 and resulted in a public punishment very similar to the beginning of *The Scarlet Letter.*
Much biographical information on various members of the
Manning family is presented and the availability of
this information to Hawthorne noted. Contradicts
earlier claims that Hawthorne was little affected by
his maternal ancestors.

381. Erlich, Gloria Chasson. "Race and Incest in Mann's
'Blood of the Walsungs.'" *Studies in Twentieth
Century Literature* 2 (1978): 113-126.

Considers the use of the incest theme in Thomas Mann's
novella, "The Blood of the Walsungs." Changes in the
ending to the story which emphasize the "Jewish situa
tion in early twentieth-century Germany" are also discussed. Mann's continued use of the incest theme in
The Holy Sinner is noted and the two works compared.
Contends that both used the incestuous relationships
to demonstrate that "the chosen of God must experience
deep sin before his special work can be done." Differences in "aesthetic distance" in Mann's treatment of
the incest theme are recognized.

382. Flinker, Noam. "Cinyras, Myrrha, and Adonis: Father-
Daughter Incest from Ovid to Milton." *Milton Studies*
14 (1980): 59-74.

Traces the use of a specific incest motif, the tale
of Myrrha's incestuous relationship with Cinyras, her
father, and the resulting birth of Adonis, written by
Ovid in his *Metamorphoses.* The handling of this story
by various authors through the seventeenth century is
examined. In some cases, the incest is negated through

"rationalizing allegorical explanations," but other
authors, like Dante, clearly labeled Myrrha as evil.
British references to Myrrha's incest in the sixteenth
and seventeenth centuries are noted. Examines in some
detail the "striking parallels between the infernal
trinity in *Paradise Lost* and Ovid's account of Myrrha's
passion for her father."

383.   Flinker, Noam. "Father-Daughter Incest in *Paradise
       Lost.*" *Milton Quarterly* 14 (December 1980): 116-122.

       Notes that descriptions of Hell in *Paradise Lost* are
       intended as "parodic imitations of Heaven" and that
       Satan's incest with his daughter, Sin, to produce Death
       is a further "parody of the trinity." References to
       father-daughter incest in Milton's *Paradise Lost* are
       identified and parallels with Satan's incest examined.
       For example, the story of Thammuz-Adonis, born of in-
       cestuous parents, is shown to be a "parallel to Death,
       infernal fruit of the union of Satan and Sin." Con-
       cludes that "what began as innocent sympathy on the
       reader's part for some of the fallen angels, should
       finally revert to a deeper sense of the reality of evil,
       at least in the mind of the Christian reader Milton
       envisioned."

384.   Furness, Raymond. "The Androgynous Ideal: Its Signifi-
       cance in German Literature." *Modern Language Review*
       60 (January 1965): 58-64.

       Traces the history of the concept of "androgynous
       unity" and applies it to modern German literature.
       Common literary, philosophical, and religious beliefs
       concerning androgyny are discussed. Notes that "andro-
       gyny is a state of perfection, that the androgyne is a
       harmonious entity in which all dissonances are resolved,
       that separation and differentiation are a curse and
       fusion and similarity a blessing." Concludes that the
       theme of incest and the androgyne are considered more
       of an ideal in "an age whose literature stresses the
       ultimate loneliness of each individual, the impossibili-
       ty of significant human relationships and the almost
       inevitable disillusionment of sexual love."

385.   Gajdusek, R.E. "Death, Incest, and the Triple Bond in
       the Later Plays of Shakespeare." *American Imago: A*

Psychoanalytic Journal for Culture, Science, and the Arts 31 (Summer 1974): 109-158.

Traces various patterns of death and incest in the later plays of Shakespeare. Contends that an in-depth study of literary allusions to incest reveals the source of the incest taboo itself. The incest taboo is seen as the "fundamental panhumanistic metaphor for regression to the original state of undifferentiated unconsciousness in uroboric inversion in the womb of the Great Mother." Detailed literary references are provided.

386. Hays, Peter L. "The Incest Theme in *Invisible Man*." *Western Humanities Review* 23 (Autumn 1969): 335-339.

Labels Ralph Ellison's *Invisible Man* a "bildungsroman, a novel about the development of an unnamed innocent" and discusses the second episode of the novel which deals with the revelation of a case of father-daughter incest. Demonstrates that the incest motif is used to signify what occurs when anyone uses a relative or member of the same race for his own purpose. Concludes that "Ellison has used incest as a shaping and controlling metaphor for interpersonal and interracial relations in the novel." The plot of the novel is recounted in some detail.

387. Homan, Sidney R., Jr. "Shakespeare and Dekker as Keys to Ford's *'Tis Pity She's a Whore*." *Studies in English Literature* 7 (Spring 1967): 269-276.

Points out similarities and differences between John Ford's *'Tis Pity She's a Whore* and two other plays, Shakespeare's *Romeo and Juliet* and *The Witch of Edmonton*, written by Ford in collaboration with William Rowley and Thomas Dekker. Plots of all three plays are summarized and minutely compared. The use of incest as the crime which violates the accepted moral code in *'Tis Pity She's a Whore* is discussed and reactions by the critics to this story of incestuous love noted. Concludes that in *'Tis Pity She's a Whore* Ford had "either reversed or complicated the notions of human responsibility which inform the early Shakespearean tragedy and the collaboration of 1621 that both directly and indirectly influenced him."

388. Kimball, Jean. "James Joyce and Otto Rank: The Incest
      Motif in *Ulysses*." *James Joyce Quarterly* 13
      (Spring 1976): 366-382.

      Examines James Joyce's use of the incest motif in
      Ulysses. Notes specific similarities between certain
      characteristics and plot elements in the novel and the
      contemporary psychological theories of Otto Rank.
      Rank's book, *The Incest Motif in Poetry and Saga:
      Fundamentals of a Psychology of Poetic Creation*, was
      published in 1912 and dealt with the Freudian analysis
      of artistic creativity. Concludes that the incest
      theme in *Ulysses* "plays a more varied and significant
      role in *Ulysses* than has generally been supposed, and
      the correspondence between theoretical observations in
      Rank's *Incest Motif* and the Hamlet theory in *Ulysses*
      suggest that Joyce was fully conscious of this role."

389. Manning, Sylvia. "Incest and the Structure of *Henry
      Esmond*." *Nineteenth-Century Fiction* 34 (September
      1979): 194-213.

      Acknowledges the basic incestuous plot elements in
      Thackeray's *Henry Esmond* and attempts to "unpack the
      incest motif from the narrative—to illustrate its
      workings throughout the novel—stopping short of the
      biographical speculation that might follow." The
      "doubling" of characters and roles is noted and the
      autobiographical form of the novel discussed. The plot
      is summarized and various incestuous relationships and
      illusions identified. Concludes that the novel must be
      read "as a display of multiple, redundant, and logically
      contradictory projections from a single, self-defeating
      fantasy of incestuous triumph."

390. Mitchell, Giles. "Incest, Demonism, and Death in
      Wuthering Heights." *Literature and Psychology* 23
      (1973): 27-36.

      Discusses the use and relationship of the incest and
      demon motifs in Emily Brontë's *Wuthering Heights*. Ana-
      lyzes Heathcliff's Satanism to "show its relationship,
      working through lycanthropic and necrophilic symptoms,
      to the incest problem." Further contends that "Heath-
      cliff's and Cathy's unconscious feelings for each other
      are ruled by incestuous desire and guilt." Numerous
      examples of these incestuous feelings and references
      to demonism are provided. Heathcliff's character is
      also viewed in "clinical terms" and related to Freudian

theories. The use of the incest motif by other
writers, e.g., Shakespeare and Dostoevsky, is
briefly noted.

391. Mitchell, Giles, and Eugene P. Wright. "Duke Ferdinand's Lycanthropy as a Disguise Motive in Webster's
The Duchess of Malfi." *Literature and Psychology* 25
(1975): 117-123.

Shows the relationship between incestuous feelings
and lycanthropy, the exhibiting of wolf-like characteristics, as used in John Webster's *The Duchess of Malfi.*
The plot is summarized to show how the main character,
Ferdinand, is affected by not only lycanthropy, but
also necrophilia because of his unconscious incestuous
attraction to his sister. Concludes that necrophilia
is "invariably and fundamentally incestuous in nature,
as indeed lycanthropy itself seems to be." Contends
that these elements of incest and supernatural traits
account for the "lurid power" of *The Duchess of Malfi.*

392. Monsarrat, Gilles D. "Unity of John Ford: *'Tis Pity
She's a Whore* and *Christ's Bloody Sweat.*" *Studies in
Philology* 77 (Summer 1980): 247-270.

Uses an early, long, religious poem by John Ford,
Christ's Bloody Sweat, to investigate the themes presented in his later play, *'Tis Pity She's a Whore.*
Each work is considered a "study in damnation." Passages are quoted from each and compared to demonstrate
how the play develops and enlarges several themes initially presented in the poem. The significance of incest as the sin which violates the moral norm is
stressed. Notes that the poem is "not used to reduce
the play to a theological scheme, but, on the contrary,
to bring out the complexity of the characters." Reaction to this "baffling play" has often depended on
the reader's own opinion of incest.

393. Pollard, Patrick. "Incest and 'Sin' in Gide's *Oedipe*
and *Les Faux-Monnayeurs.*" *Nottingham French Studies*
19 (October 1980): 25-30.

Analyzes two works by André Gide to determine how
they deal with the following moral questions: "the
dependence of the child on its inherited situation;
autonomy and individuality; the possibility of revolt;
the acting out by a new generation of desires which for
the older, can only remain unfulfilled." The incest

motif, specifically the story of Oedipe's incestuous
relationship with Jocaste, is used in the play *Oedipe*
to "explore the moral dilemma in which Man finds him-
self vis-a-vis established religion." Gide's only
novel *Les Faux-Monnayeurs* is the other work considered,
but incest is not involved in the plot.

394. Prigozy, Ruth. "From Griffith's Girls to Daddy's
      Girl: The Masks of Innocence in *Tender Is the Night*."
      Twentieth Century Literature 26 (Summer 1980): 189-221.

      Describes how F. Scott Fitzgerald's *Tender Is the
      Night* "traces American history through the central
      metaphor of the novel, the incestuous father-daughter
      relationship, actual in the Warren family and mythic in
      the title and scenario of Rosemary Hoyt's great Holly-
      wood success, *Daddy's Girl*." Notes that both his own
      role as a father and popular culture caused Fitzgerald
      to use the theme of incest. An overview of "daddy's
      girls" as presented in silent films, especially those
      of D.W. Griffith, is given and "Fitzgerald's debt to
      the 'daddy's girls' in real life and in popular culture"
      emphasized.

395. Rapf, Joanna E. "Byronic Heroine: Incest and the
      Creative Process." *Studies in English Literature* 21
      (Autumn 1981): 637-645.

      Analyzes the portrayal of women in the poetry of Lord
      Byron. Notes that for Byron the "ideal woman had to be
      that which was closest to himself, of the same blood,
      flesh, spirit: a sister." Since any relationship with
      this type of woman would be incestuous and socially un-
      acceptable, Byron's treatment of women is generally
      "disdainful." Concludes that, "unable to accept the
      female side of the creative process, fearing it as in-
      cestuous, he turned to humor, making fun of the intensi-
      ty of the human search for love."

396. Rosenblatt, Jason P. "Aspects of the Incest Problems
      in *Hamlet*." *Shakespeare Quarterly* 29 (Summer 1978):
      349-364.

      Notes that various ethical or psychological approaches
      have been applied to *Hamlet*, particularly as they focus
      on the relationship between Gertrude, Claudius and
      Hamlet. Employs a religious interpretation on this re-
      lationship, noting that Hamlet's grievance against
      Claudius is based on a text in Leviticus; Claudius'

defense is based on a text in Deuteronomy. Draws
parallels to the historical and religious conflicts
which arise when Henry VIII decided to divorce Catherine
of Aragon and marry Anne Boleyn. Argues that an understanding of orthodox religious interpretations in the
sixteenth century helps the reader understand Claudius'
guilt and Hamlet's distress.

397. See, F.G. "Kinship of Metaphor--Incest and Language in
     Melville's *Pierre*." *Structuralist Review* 1 (1978):
     55-81.

     Considers the use of the incest theme in Herman Mel-
     ville's *Pierre*. Traces the plot of the novel and
     demonstrates how language, especially puns and metaphors,
     is used to introduce the hero's eventual involvement in
     an incestuous relationship. Summarizes the theories of
     Lévi-Strauss concerning kinship and how they "suggest a
     connection between language and incest which may help
     to illuminate Melville's deliberate excesses of lan-
     guage." The use of the incest theme and the overall
     style of the novel clearly troubled earlier reviewers.
     Notes that this is also because "the mythic tradition
     which romanticism uses to express and verify its uni-
     verse may be understood to fall into fragments following
     Pierre's violation of the incest taboo."

398. Sundquist, Eric J. "Incest and Imitation in Cooper's
     Home As Found." *Nineteenth-Century Fiction* 32
     (December 1977): 261-284.

     Argues that the question of incest in James Fenimore
     Cooper's *Home As Found* cannot be dismissed as incidental
     but must be considered an essential component of the
     novel. The possible autobiographic nature of the story
     is considered, and the novel is briefly compared to
     Cooper's earlier, more famous works. Concludes that
     his treatment of incest is "intimately tied to the pe-
     culiarly American question of imitation and its rela-
     tion to social and literary authority." The plot is
     summarized and passages are cited to support this con-
     clusion.

399. Thomas, Brook. "The Writer's Procreative Urge in *Pierre*:
     Fictional Freedom or Convoluted Incest?" *Studies in
     the Novel* 11 (Winter 1979): 416-430.

     Explores the use of the "human/artistic procreation
     metaphor" in Herman Melville's *Pierre*. Specific ex-

amples and passages from *Pierre* and other Melville
novels are cited to investigate the belief of many
nineteenth century writers that "artistic procreation
is incestuous." Concludes that the metaphor of incest
"accounts for both the difference necessary for the
creative act and the continual reduplication of personality (repetition) that no artist can avoid, for in
incest we make love to someone of the opposite sex in
whom we see ourselves mirrored." Notes, however, that
Pierre "remains ambiguous to the end."

400. Trainer, James. "The Incest-Theme in the Works of
      Tieck." *Modern Language Notes* 76 (December 1961):
      819-824.

      Studies the use of the incest motif in the works of
      Ludwig Tieck. Does not attempt to detemine what per-
      sonal relations might have caused Tieck to repeatedly
      use this theme. Various works of his are cited and the
      uses of the incest motif noted. Contends that in several
      al cases the incest content is "purely theatrical, if
      not actually ridiculous." Also discusses authors,
      specifically Horace Walpole and M.G. Lewis, whose use
      of incest may have influenced Tieck. Concludes that
      "Tieck had ample literary precedence for employing it
      and the question whether personal tensions helped to
      promote this interest will be better left to psycholo-
      gists."

401. Turner, Gordon. "The Incest Bond in Stead's *Grain*."
      The Sphinx: A Magazine of Literature and Society 2
      (Winter 1977): 23-32.

      Considers the incestuous attraction the main charac-
      ter in Robert J.C. Stead's novel, *Grain*, has for his
      sister. The plot is summarized in great detail and the
      significance of this incestuous attraction, although it
      was never consumated, is stressed. Concludes that this
      incest motif is used to analyze the "sexual immaturity
      which is a by-product of the close familial ties in
      pioneer prairie households where obeisance to contin-
      ence was unwritten law."

402. Twitchell, James. "The Incest Theme and the Authentici-
      ty of the Percy Version of 'Edward.'" *Western
      Folklore* 34 (January 1975): 32-35.

      Investigates the authenticity of the Percy version of
      "Edward." The repeated use of incest as the theme of

various other Domestic Tragedy ballads is noted.
Generally only sibling incest is portrayed. Seen in
the context of these other ballads which use sibling
incest as the theme, the Percy Version of "Edward" is
considered authentic because it is the only version
that does not involve maternal incest.

403. Wilson, James D. "Incest and American Romantic Fiction."
      Studies in the Literary Imagination 7 (Spring 1974):
      31-50.

      Provides an overview of the use of sibling incest as
      a theme in the works of "American dark Romantics."
      Contends that sibling incest is used as a symbol of
      solipsism and used to "portray self-absorption as the
      avenue to dementia and eventual destruction." The
      following are considered: William Hill Brown's *The Power
      of Sympathy*, Charles Brockden Brown's *Wieland*, Haw-
      thorne's "Alice Doane's Appeal," and Melville's *Pierre*.

VIII

AV MATERIALS

404. "Audio-Digest Psychiatry, Volume 6, Number 14: Incest:
Fantasy and Fact." Audiocassette (60 minutes).
Audio-Digest Foundation, 1577 E. Chevy Chase Dr.,
Glendale, CA 91206.

Consists of papers read at the meeting of the American Psychiatric Association and the American Society of
Adolescent Psychiatry in 1977. Designed for professionals involved in the treatment and investigation of incest cases. Includes discussions of incest occurrence,
investigative techniques, therapy and case studies of
incestuous families. (*Child Abuse and Neglect*, National
Center on Child Abuse and Neglect's database, Fall 1980
edition)

405. "The 'C' Case." (1977) Color, 3/4" videocassette (40
minutes). Midwest Parent-Child Welfare Resource
Center, University of Wisconsin, Milwaukee, WI 53201.

Studies the dynamics of father-daughter incest in a
fictionalized encounter between a counselor and a young
woman. Psychological aspects of the father and daughter
are explored. Notes the daughter's confusion over the
relationship and the father's marital difficulties.
The possibility of family therapy is proposed. (*Child
Abuse and Neglect*, Fall 1980 edition)

406. "Childhood Sexual Abuse." Color, 16mm film (50 minutes).
Cavalcade Productions. Distributor: Motorola Teleprograms, 4825 N. Scott St., Schiller Park, IL 60176.

Examines the experiences and feelings of four female
victims of childhood sexual abuse. Cases are revealed
in detail through the women's presentations in group
therapy. (*Child Abuse and Neglect*, Fall 1980 edition)

143

407. "Incest: The Broken Silence." (1978) Color, 3/4" video-
      cassette (30 minutes). Junior League of San Diego.
      Distributor: KPBS-TV, San Diego State University,
      San Diego, CA 92182.

      Focuses on the issue of father-daughter incest through
      the testimony of family participants and health profes-
      sionals. Discusses causes and effects of incest and
      the possible treatment of family members with attention
      paid to reestablishing the family unit. (*Child Abuse
      and Neglect*, Fall 1980 edition)

408. "Incest: The Hidden Crime." Color, 16mm film (28 min-
      utes). Media Guild Solona Beach, California. Dis-
      tributor: Howard University, Region III Child Abuse
      and Neglect Resource Center, 2900 Van Ness St. N.W.,
      Washington, D.C. 20008.

      Explores how family members cope with the disclosure
      of father-daughter incest. Designed for use by health
      professionals for training. General information on in-
      cestuous relations in the family is also presented.
      (*Child Abuse and Neglect*, Fall 1981 edition)

409. "Incest: The Last Word in Taboos." (1972) Audiocassette
      (30 minutes). CBC Learning Systems, Box 500, Terminal
      A, Toronto, Ontario 116.

      Explores the life of a woman who had experienced a
      past incestuous relationship. (*NICEM Media Index*, 1979
      edition)

410. "Incest: The Victim Nobody Believes." (1976) Color,
      16mm film (20 minutes). Mitchell-Gebhardt Film Co.,
      1380 Bush St., San Francisco, CA 94109.

      Recounts the experiences of three victims of father-
      daughter incest. Their feelings and reactions to the
      events are explored and the coping mechanisms employed
      are examined. Frequency, causes, and treatment of
      incest are emphasized in an accompanying study guide.
      (*Child Abuse and Neglect*, Fall 1980 edition; NCJRS *Docu-
      ment Retrieval Index*, 1972-78)

411. "It Only Happens Next Door." (1977) Color, 3/4" video-
      cassette (35 minutes). National Broadcasting Company.
      Distributor: Films Inc., 1144 Wilmette Ave., Wilmette,
      IL 60091.

      Focuses on the incidence, effects and treatment of
      incest victims, particularly children. Actual victims

of incest present their experiences in the therapeutic
setting of the Child Sexual Abuse Treatment Center of
Santa Clara County, California. (*Child Abuse and
Neglect*, Fall 1981 edition)

412. "The Last Taboo." (1977) Color, 16mm film (30 minutes).
Cavalcade Productions. Distributor: Motorola Teleprograms, 4825 N. Scott St., Schiller Park, IL 60176.

Presents six adult women who were victims of sexual
abuse as children as they discuss their experiences in
group therapy. Explores the abusive situation from the
child's perspective and reveals how these experiences
influence the individuals throughout their lives.
Methods for therapeutic treatment are discussed.
(*Child Abuse and Neglect*, Fall 1980 edition)

413. McCulley, D. "Double Jeopardy." (1978) Color, 16mm
film (40 minutes). University of Washington, Cavalcade Productions. Distributor: Motorola Teleprograms,
4825 N. Scott St., Suite 23, Schiller Park, IL 60176.

Explores the complex process of dealing with the victim of incest and effectively providing support and
legal protection. Points out that victims are often
treated insensitively by health professional and law
enforcement personnel. Discusses the techniques for
interviewing children in a way that does not traumatize
them and for preparing children to give testimony
during judicial proceedings. (National Criminal Justice
Reference Service *Document Retrieval Index*, 1979 Supplement)

414. "Nobody Told Me: Sexual Abuse of Children." (1978)
Audiocassette (29 minutes). Feminist Radio Network,
P.O. Box 5536, Washington, D.C. 20016.

Covers the broad topic of sexual abuse of children
with particular emphasis on the activities of the
Christopher Street Project in Minneapolis which deals
with adolescents and adults who are or were victims of
incest. Individuals involved in the incest and investi-
gators present their attitudes and approaches to the
problem. (*Child Abuse and Neglect*, Fall 1980 edition)

415. Robinson, R. "Child Abuse." (1977) Color, 16mm film
(29 minutes). U.S. Department of Justice Law Enforcement Assistance Administration. Distributor: AIMS

Instructional Media Inc., 626 Justine Ave.,
Glendale, CA 91201

Deals with three different types of child abuse
situations: battered children, father-daughter incest,
and wanton neglect. Section on incest provides information in several areas including (1) effects of incest,
i.e., drug abuse, suicide, prostitution; (2) the power
of warrantless search and seizure; and (3) admissibility
of testimony during judicial procedures. Directed
toward individuals involved in law enforcement. (National Criminal Justice Reference Service *Document Retrieval Index*, 1979 Supplement)

416. "Sexual Abuse." (1976) Audiocassette (24 minutes).
      Protective Services Resource Institute, Rutgers
      Medical School, P.O. Box 101, Piscataway, NJ 08854.

      Presents three convicted child molesters from Rahway
      State Prison who discuss the characteristics of the
      incest perpetrator with the director of the Adult Diag-
      nostic Center in Avenal, New Jersey. Reviews methods
      of helping the child victim understand what has happened
      and how to perceive the offender. (*Child Abuse and
      Neglect*, Fall 1980 edition)

417. "Sexual Abuse: The Family." (1976) Color, 16mm film
      (25 minutes). National Center on Child Abuse and
      Neglect, Washington, D.C. Distributor: National
      Audiovisual Center, GSA, Order Section, Washington,
      D.C. 20409.

      Provides a general discussion of many aspects of the
      incestuous family. Among the areas discussed are the
      physical and psychological characteristics of family
      members, the family environment and interaction, inter-
      view techniques, and treatment approaches. Maintaining
      the integrity of the family is identified as an impor-
      tant goal in the treatment process. (*Child Abuse and
      Neglect*, Fall and May 1980 edition)

418. "Shatter the Silence." (1981) Color, 16mm film (29 min-
      utes). S-L Film Productions, Los Angeles, California.
      Distributor: Phoenix Films, Inc., 468 Park Ave. S.,
      New York, NY 10016

      Explores the family dynamics of father-daughter incest
      through a dramatization. Characteristics noted include
      job loss and consequent insecurity of the father, with-
      drawal of affection and isolation of the mother, and

transference of mother/wife roles to the daughter. Group therapy as treatment is also explored. (*Child Abuse and Neglect*, Fall 1981 edition)

419. "We Can Help: Unit 6: Identifying the Sexually Abused Child." (1976) Color, 16mm film (25 minutes). National Center on Child Abuse and Neglect, Washington, D.C. Distributor: National Audiovisual Center, GSA, Order Section, Washington, D.C. 20409.

Explores family and individual characteristics of incest participants and the social attitudes toward incest. Emphasis is on trainees' attitudes toward both the victim and the victimizer. Part of a training program which includes this film. (*Child Abuse and Neglect*, Fall 1980 edition)

PERIODICALS CITED

AUTHOR INDEX

SUBJECT INDEX

Subject Index

Effects of incest—Short term
58, 86, 115, 116, 118, 122,
126, 138, 172, 218, 319,
331
Effigy hangings 286
Ego function 173
Egypt 66, 270, 278, 295
Elementary Structure of Kin-
ship 287
Ellison, Ralph 386
Emergency room 326
Endogamous incest 146, 252
Eros 73
European literature 379
See also Incest in
literature
Evidence 318, 340
Evolution 24, 327
Exogamy 24, 264, 267, 272,
273, 276, 277, 284, 288,
290, 294, 296

False accusation. See
Accusation
Fantasies 170
Families Reunited 134
Family's role 1, 4, 5, 6, 7,
12, 20, 21, 22, 27, 29, 31,
34, 35, 37, 38, 39, 44, 46,
52, 65, 75, 78, 92, 95, 99,
102, 108, 115, 123, 128,
129, 131, 134, 140, 142,
143, 144, 146, 147, 149,
152, 156, 161, 165, 169,
174, 178, 186, 187, 188,
196, 198, 205, 206, 210,
218, 232, 235, 236, 242,
244, 251, 254, 259, 304,
308, 312, 328, 334, 346,
350, 357, 405, 407, 408,
417, 418, 419
Family practitioner. See
Physicians
Family reunion 35, 156, 220,
407
Family separation 5, 110,
116, 187, 232, 417

Family therapy 35, 42, 81,
97, 99, 110, 121, 237
Family violence 250
Father-daughter incest 1, 2,
3, 4, 5, 8, 20, 21, 22, 27,
28, 29, 31, 33, 37, 46, 50,
54, 62, 67, 74, 78, 81, 83,
87, 90, 91, 103, 110, 111,
122, 127, 128, 129, 140,
142, 144, 145, 158, 164,
167, 168, 169, 173, 177,
185, 200, 204, 205, 206,
207, 211, 212, 215, 217,
223, 225, 227, 239, 240,
254, 310, 321, 334, 342,
346, 355, 359, 364, 365,
367, 383, 386, 394, 405,
407, 408, 410, 415, 418
Father-son incest 46, 98,
123, 144
Father's role 8, 17, 22, 29,
37, 39, 44, 54, 128, 158,
204, 207, 212, 218, 242,
249, 254, 256, 342, 365,
405, 418, 419
Les Faux-Monnayeurs 393
Feminism 24, 32, 49, 205,
207, 221, 362
Fertility 317
Fielding, Henry 376
Fielding, Sarah 376
Filicide 107, 283
Films (audiovisual materials)
406, 408, 412, 413, 415,
417, 418, 419
Films (theatrical). See
Movies
Finkelhor, David 351
Fitzgerald, F. Scott 395
Flesh and Blood 372
Folklore 60, 261, 280, 374,
402
Food exogamy 276
Forced sex. See Coercive sex
Ford, John 14, 72, 387, 399
Foster parents 172
French literature 393. See
also Incest in literature